'Explosions, speed, motion, beauty, wonder, colour, transformation, amazement... what's not to like about science?'

BRF's Messy Church has been embraced wholeheartedly by many local churches, and through it we have the opportunity, as well as the creative imagination and energy, to bring science into the way we 'do church'. We can help the subject become an accepted and expected part of worship and learning, and a means by which we can meet God and learn to love the natural world.

Messy Churches are hot on discovery, experimentation and exploration; could we encourage even more Messy Church groups to feel confident about using science in the activity time, so that families would understand that the church celebrates science and rejoices in it?

Lucy Moore, founder of Messy Church

Find out more about our Messy Church Does Science initiative, and download additional resources, at **messychurch.org.uk/science**

The Bible Reading Fellowship
15 The Chambers, Vineyard
Abingdon OX14 3FE
brf.org.uk

The Bible Reading Fellowship (BRF) is a Registered Charity (233280)

ISBN 978 0 85746 579 5
First published 2017
Reprinted 2017
10 9 8 7 6 5 4 3 2 1
All rights reserved

Text © individual authors 2017
With additional material provided by David Gregory and Lucy Moore
This edition © The Bible Reading Fellowship 2017
Illustrations by Rebecca J Hall

Acknowledgements
Unless otherwise stated, scripture quotations are taken from The Holy
Bible, New International Version (Anglicised edition) copyright © 1979, 1984,
2011 by Biblica. Used by permission of Hodder & Stoughton Publishers, an
Hachette UK company. All rights reserved. 'NIV' is a registered trademark of
Biblica. UK trademark number 1448790.

Extracts from the Authorised Version of the Bible (The King James Bible), the
rights in which are vested in the Crown, are reproduced by permission of the
Crown's Patentee, Cambridge University Press.

Scripture quotations taken from the Holy Bible, New Living Translation,
copyright © 1996, 2004, 2007, 2013. Used by permission of Tyndale House
Publishers, Inc., Carol Stream, Illinois 60188. All rights reserved.

Scripture quotations from The New Revised Standard Version of the Bible,
Anglicised edition, copyright © 1989, 1995 by the Division of Christian
Education of the National Council of the Churches of Christ in the United
States of America. Used by permission. All rights reserved.

Every effort has been made to trace and contact copyright owners for
material used in this resource. We apologise for any inadvertent omissions
or errors, and would ask those concerned to contact us so that full
acknowledgement can be made in the future.

A catalogue record for this book is available from the British Library

Printed and bound by Gutenberg Press, Tarxien, Malta

does
science

100 si**z**zli**ng** science-based
ideas for Messy Churches

Edited by **David Gregory**

For Andrew Hall
In slight resentment that you got all the science genes,
but with much love.
Lucy Moore

To my Mum and Dad
who bought me my first telescope so I could look at
the stars and then gaze beyond creation.
David Gregory

Acknowledgements

We would like to thank Scientists in Congregations (**www.scientistsincongregations.org**) for the generous grant that has made this project possible.

We are very grateful to the Messy Churches who offered to field test these experiments. Their feedback, comments and enthusiasm were invaluable in making this book.

Contents

Introduction

Messy Church does science?

Maybe that was the question you asked yourself when you first came across this book. I mean, what does science have to do with church anyhow? Faith and science just don't mix. And if they do, well, it's a bit explosive! That's the impression you might have got from listening to a lot of voices in the media and perhaps church too. But maybe there's another way of looking at it; a way that sees science fitting into what George Lings in *Messy Church Theology* (BRF, 2013) describes as the DNA of Messy Church – 'hospitality, creativity and celebration'.

That's an interesting choice of words. The oft-used phrase 'DNA' reveals just how much science talk has slipped into the way we describe and see the world. We may not understand precisely what DNA is in scientific terms – the chemical that is at the heart of all life on earth, including nearly every cell of our bodies – but we at least have a sense that it defines in part who we are; what colour eyes or hair you have, and whether you look a little like your Nana Ethel! Yet despite this use of scientific language in our culture and even within the life of the church, science is not always something that finds a welcome within church life. We lose something because of that, for it is just as much a part of human creativity as art, music and drama – a gift from God, expressing what it means to be human and allowing us to explore creation and perhaps catch a glimpse of the creator.

Messy Church doing science

My own journey into the world of science began when I was five or six in the mid-1960s. At school we watched a black and white TV broadcast of what must have been a Gemini rocket launch – the precursor to the Apollo moon landing programme. These events of my pre-teen years got me firmly interested in science, initially space and astronomy, and eventually led me into a career in weather and climate science. Maybe it was the start of my own journey that enabled me to listen to the voice of a six-year-old who said, 'You're Dr Dave. I can't wait until I am old enough to come to the Messy Science Lab.'

She had been coming along to our Messy Church for a while where, like a few other Messy Churches, we had been offering simple science experiments to some of the older children who were a bit bored with the usual craft activities. Seeing this young girl's excitement over joining in the experiments, we opened up the lab to the younger children. Now, each month ten to fifteen families with children aged from five to ten come along to the 'Messy Science Lab' led by Dr Dave in his white scientist coat.

A recent survey across the Messy Church network reveals that this journey parallels the experience of others who are using science as part of their local Messy Church. You don't have to know a lot about science to do this. People running the science experiments have a range of scientific expertise – from very little training up to those engaged in research. Our hope is that the experiments in this book will enable others across the family of Messy Church to have a go themselves, helping families to discover that science is welcome in the world of faith. Through its creativity, we want to enable families to enjoy the wonder of creation and to celebrate that wonder, encountering the one who shapes it.

The DNA of Messy Church science

So, how might science fit within the DNA of Messy Church?

Science and hospitality

Sadly for me, an interest in science from a young age meant that I did not find church very welcoming. In my teens I left church behind, only reconnecting later when I began to explore the interaction of science and faith further at university. This is the sphere of apologetics, which is often not seen as a ready fit for sharing with families and younger children. But including science within Messy Church says to these families that science is indeed welcome in the church, and that those who are fascinated by it are welcome too.

Throughout this book there are stories from scientists who are Christians detailing their own journey with science and faith. Allowing families to meet Christians who are interested in science within local Messy Churches will enable them to encounter such stories more personally. Adults coming along to the Messy Science Lab I run often express surprise that someone of faith is interested in science, challenging the popular notion that science and faith cannot fit together in a personal and relational way. This can be of real significance as people explore faith in Jesus.

Science and creativity

Church life and worship have always used music and art in helping people to encounter and express their relationship with God, sharing in the creativity of God as beings made in his image. As we grow through the education system, in our teenage years we often have to make a choice between 'arts' and 'sciences', leaving people with the feeling that they are good at one or the other. Science is often seen as a matter-of-fact exercise, explaining how things *are*. Yet it too is an activity that expresses human creativity, whether through using our skills to operate equipment to undertake an experiment, or using our senses to explore what is happening in the experiments, or using our minds to describe, question and explain. Science is a playful activity that enables us to share in the playfulness of God in creation, expressing in our lives today the story we read at the start of the book of Genesis where God invites Adam to give names to all the animals.

The important thing about science is not getting the right answer. More important is asking the right questions. I often ask the families to explain what is going on in an experiment. Explanations offered are often imaginatively creative, if not always right – but many of the explanations that science has come up with through the centuries have been wrong too! This captures the essence of science that those who work within the world of science will recognise. Messy Church science allows children and adults to grow in confidence. Children are offered the chance to discover an interest in science and begin to understand how science explores the world in a methodical way. And for adults, who perhaps left science behind in earlier years thinking it was too hard for them, it provides a second chance to discover it afresh, and perhaps an ability to enjoy science with their children as they grow. For all, it helps them to discover a little more of the people who God has made them to be, and hopefully more of who God is.

Science and celebration

Children grow up encountering science from a very young age in our culture – in school, through technology and the media, both in factual programmes about the world and imaginative science fiction. Recent research suggests that children who do not grow up with a faith often express their natural sense of spirituality in the language of science. This is often lost in young adult years when our educational system takes a more rational approach to science, stressing a separation from faith. Using science in creative ways to explore faith provides language that fits to children's wider view of the world, shaping faith and hopefully planting at least a memory that, as they grow through their young adult years, will counter the notion of the opposing natures of science and faith.

Many people who are a part of Messy Church come from unchurched backgrounds. Exploring the stories of the Bible and Jesus in creative ways is part of the way Messy Church helps people come to faith in Jesus. Each of the science experiments contains suggestions as to how they might relate to a Bible story, providing an illustration or reinforcing the core message of the session. But, as with other approaches seeking to help those unfamiliar with the traditional stories of faith – such as Godly Play – more reflective, open questions in response to the experiments will also help people to encounter God, much as many people feel a connection to something beyond themselves when they ponder the beauty of creation. Connecting what people see in the experiments to prayer is another way they can be helped to connect with God, individually and in corporate worship. This can feel a bit risky. Ideas of God arising from such reflective activities may not fully match the God who is revealed in Jesus, needing to be balanced by more direct explanation of biblical material. However, it gives space for the Holy Spirit to be at work in drawing people towards Jesus, reminding us that we are working in cooperation with God, who is present in the whole of creation and life.

Doing Messy Church science

This book offers 100 outlines of experiments under ten different topic headings. We do not suggest that you run an entire Messy Science session of ten activities at a time, unless of course you particularly wish to have a special science focus! Rather, these ideas can be selected from as desired in order to add a scientific element to the proceedings – using one or possibly two activities from the book within each session. To help you choose experiments, each comes with a 'Mess', 'Danger' and 'Difficulty' rating marked out of five. If you are unfamiliar with running science within Messy Church, we recommend you begin with some of the simpler experiments. Children are fascinated by trying experiments with their own hands and discovering something new, without them having a dramatic 'wow' factor. But do not be put off by some of the more difficult and risky experiments. Having a 'wow' factor every so often will keep their attention!

The experiments have been designed so that they can be used by people with little background in science and to fit within the timeframe of the activity section of a typical Messy Church (20–25 minutes). Each comes with a list of equipment needed, most readily available in shops or which can be found around the home and lying around a typical church. There are some that will need more specialised equipment – such as strong bar magnets, electrical cables and fittings, prisms, diffraction gratings and microscopes. These can be sourced cheaply through a variety of internet outlets.

Step-by-step instructions on how the experiment is to be carried out are also provided to help it go well, although science does not always go to plan! While the experiments have been trialled, and you are encouraged to try them for yourself before going live in a Messy Church session, at times experiments will not go as expected, often because of mistakes in following the method, but do not be discouraged. There will always be something to talk about and learn and, in any case, some of the greatest scientific advances have come about through mistakes!

In each experiment, 'Big thinking' explores in a simple way some of the science behind the activity. Some also have links to additional material on the web, which may help you understand and explain the science background of the experiment; you might want to encourage families to explore these later. Some of the experiments have additional take-home items that can be used in the celebration together, as well as allowing families to continue to explore the science and theme of the Messy Church session at home.

As you do the experiments, don't just focus upon the outcome alone. You might want to ask people why we do the experiments in a particular way or what they expect to happen – which can lead to those 'wow' moments when something different actually happens! Encourage the children to chat with family members and leaders about what they are doing and seeing, and encourage them to explain what is happening in the experiment. Remember, getting the answer right is not always the most important thing. Creativity, imagination and just having a go are. In the 'Big questions' section of each experiment there are also links to Bible stories, Christian festivals and suggestions for reflective or prayer activities. Ensure that you leave time for this – sometimes it can be easy for the excitement of the experiments to take over!

Most of these experiments are deemed to be low risk. But for some, caution is needed, especially those using heat, electricity, chemicals, bright light sources and material that might be tasted or eaten. Ensure that you think through any risk issues before using the experiment and what steps might be needed to minimise risk, such as ensuring good adult supervision. A few specific issues to be aware of:

- Some experiments require products you can find around the home that come with childproof tops – such as bleach or methylated spirits. Please read the safety information before using them. Be particularly aware of those that cause irritation to skin, airways and eyes, or are dangerous if ingested. If you use such material, it is advisable to ensure participants wear disposable vinyl gloves and keep their arms, legs and feet covered. Eye goggles are also advisable – and make sure the church's first-aid kit contains equipment for washing out eyes. Please ensure that the outcomes of such experiments are not taken home, as risk cannot be controlled once they have left the Messy Church session.
- Similarly, some experiments require more specialist chemicals which can be sourced from the internet. Some suppliers provide good safety advice with the product. Others do not, and you many need to search on the internet for health and safety advice. Again, use of disposable vinyl gloves and eye goggles is recommended and experiments should not be taken home.
- A few of the experiments involve tasting various substances. Please check possible allergy risks in these cases, as well as anywhere substances might come in contact with exposed skin.
- Do not allow children to touch equipment linked to mains electricity. All electrical equipment used should be PAT tested.
- Children and adults should not look directly at bright light sources – such as a laser source – with their eyes or through a lens. This is particularly true of looking directly at the sun, which will cause permanent damage to eyes. This is worth saying twice – NEVER LOOK AT THE SUN DIRECTLY.

If you have not done science experiments before in Messy Church, it is advisable not to try the higher-risk experiments first, no matter how tempting that might be! You could instead try them out first as a demonstration. The few experiments that are suggested as 'Demo only' are clearly marked as such under the 'Danger rating'. You should not allow children, even with adult supervision, to undertake them.

Have fun!

In the Messy Science Lab I run as part of a local Messy Church, before the families enter I remind them of the four simple lab rules:

Rule 1   Listen to Dr Dave
Rule 2   If you cannot remember rule 2, then think back to rule 1. What's that?
Rule 3   If you cannot remember rule 2 or 3, just remember rule 1! Say it again!
Rule 4   Have fun!

This has become a ritual for us at the start of each experiment, with children and adults shouting out 'Listen to Dr Dave', ramping up the volume each time. It's about sharing together in the activity as well as making sure that families are able to listen to the experimental instructions and that any 'risky' bits are done safely. But rule 4 is the most important – 'Have fun!'

Those who have contributed to the range of experiments in this book have found that science is fun, a gift from God that brings joy to life, helping us appreciate his life and love all the more. All of us want to share that sense with others, helping them to enjoy the wonder that science reveals about the world and ourselves, and through it something of the God of life who lies behind it all. We hope you will discover this for yourselves, and share it with the families of your Messy Churches as you try out the experiments, helping them to discover and share in the life that God gives us through Jesus. And remember – 'Have fun!'

Dr Dave

Dave Gregory

View or download photos and videos of the activities
in this book at **messychurch.org.uk/science**

1

Water

 After being a maths teacher for seven years, **Kate Toogood** moved to Oxford to train for ordination and is currently serving her curacy in Louth, where she is also completing an MA in Theology and Ministry. Kate is the Messy Church coordinator in Louth and, after developing a keen interest in 'Science and Faith' discussions, introduced science activities as part of their regular structure. Kate will soon be taking up a joint position as Associate Chaplain and teacher at Reading Blue Coat School, and Associate Vicar at St Andrew's, Sonning, in the Diocese of Oxford. She is married to Lawrence and they have three sons.

Introduction

Water is something which we see throughout the Bible; from the beginning of creation, through the parting of the Red Sea, to the baptism of Jesus, water is full of significance and symbolism for Christians. The activities in this chapter all involve water and so are appropriate for any water-related theme or story. However, by looking more deeply at how we can link these experiments to our understanding of God, these water-based activities can be used to demonstrate a wide range of Christian themes and motifs, linking to a wide spectrum of Bible verses.

It will come as no surprise that the activities in this chapter may get you (and others) wet! It is certainly worth making sure that these activities are carried out somewhere where spillage would not cause damage, and have a dry towel nearby!

Water-related stories include the story of creation in Genesis 1, Noah's Ark, Isaac and Rebekah at the well, the Nile in the ten plagues of Egypt, crossing the Red Sea, the waters of Meribah (Numbers 20), crossing the Jordan (Joshua 4),

Ezekiel's vision of the temple (Ezekiel 47), Jonah, Psalm 23 'the still waters' and many other psalms, John the Baptist, Jesus' baptism, Jesus turning water into wine, calling his followers beside the Sea of Galilee, or preaching from the boat, calming the storm, walking on water, causing the pigs to jump in the lake, talking to the woman at the well, healing at the pool of Siloam, living water (John 7), the Ethiopian official (Acts 8), the river in John's vision (Revelation 22).

Floating and sinking eggs

Ratings

MESS ☐☐☐☐☐   DANGER ☐☐☐☐☐   DIFFICULTY ☐☐☐☐☐

Theme

God's strength

Equipment needed

Beakers or glasses of water; eggs; salt

Before you begin

You will need plenty of salt, so make sure it is in good supply, especially if you let each participant have their own glass of water.

For visual effectiveness, it works well if you choose two eggs of a similar size.

Experimental method

Place an egg in a beaker of cold water and watch what happens: the egg sinks. Add five tablespoons of salt to a beaker of water and stir until the salt is mixed in well. Now very gently place an egg inside this beaker – the egg now floats.

Big thinking

Why does the egg float? This activity is about density; salt water is denser (heavier) than ordinary tap water and this causes the egg to float. Can you think of any other examples where the density of water affects whether things float? A good example you could give is the Dead Sea, one of the world's saltiest bodies of water. Because there is so much salt in the Dead Sea, it is dense enough that even people float!

Big questions

What do we need in *our* lives to uphold us? We are told in the Bible of the importance and enormity of God's strength and how we can be upheld by God, perhaps during challenging times when our own strength is not enough. What could we add to our lives which would help to further strengthen and uphold us?

How can we support each other, perhaps through prayer and helping each other in times when we feel our own strength isn't enough?

The Bible has many references to the strength of God, such as in the letter to the Ephesians where we are told to 'be strong in the Lord' (Ephesians 6:10). Other relevant Bible verses include Isaiah 40:29, Philippians 4:13 and 2 Corinthians 12:9–10.

This activity can also be linked to Old Testament stories set around the Dead Sea, such as the story of Naomi. It could also link to the theme of salt, such as 'You are the salt of the earth' (Matthew 5:13).

Tornado in a bottle

Ratings

MESS 💡💡🔅🔅🔅 DANGER 💡🔅🔅🔅🔅 DIFFICULTY 💡💡💡🔅🔅

Theme

The peace of God

Equipment needed

Water; plastic bottles; washing-up liquid; colourful glitter (optional)

Before you begin

This experiment looks simple but it can be tricky to get right, so if you don't succeed the first time – don't give up!

Experimental method

Fill a plastic bottle about three-quarters of the way up with cold water. Add a couple of drops of washing-up liquid and some glitter (if you would like) to the bottle and put the lid on tightly. Gently turn the bottle upside down and, holding the bottle by the lid, turn it using a big circular motion. Look in the centre and you should see a mini tornado. Try not to shake the bottle too much as this makes the appearance of the tornado less effective.

Big thinking

Why does the water look like a tornado? As you swirl the bottle round in a circular motion, the water flows in a circle around the bottle and so is pushed to the side by a centrifugal force – the same way you are pushed to the side as you are spun on a roundabout. The air then swirls into the centre and the tornado appears.

Big questions

What do we do when things unsettle us? In God we are promised a peace that the world cannot give, a peace that we can feel both in the joys and in the difficulties of life. We read in the Bible about God's peace (Psalm 29:11, Philippians 4:7), and there are also a number of Bible stories about unsettling storms, a good example being the Gospel story where Jesus stilled the storm (Mark 4:35–41). Even in the midst of a storm, we can find a peace that comes from God. What storms do we have in our lives? When things unsettle us, we too can pray for God's peace.

Other Bible stories with storms include Elijah and the still small voice (1 Kings 19), Job, Jonah, Paul's shipwreck (Acts 27).

Wave machine

Ratings

MESS   DANGER   DIFFICULTY

Theme

Creation

Equipment needed

Water; plastic bottles; blue food colouring; vegetable oil

Before you begin

Remember that oil can be messy, so it may be a good idea to have some kitchen paper close by in case of spillages.

Experimental method

Pour a cup of water into the bottle, add a few drops of blue food colouring and then a cup of vegetable oil, and put the lid on the bottle. Place the bottle on its side and the liquids will separate, with the oil on top. Tip the bottle gently backwards and forwards to create waves.

Big thinking

Why do the liquids separate? They separate because of their different densities; oil is less dense than water and so the oil will sit on top of the water. Have you ever noticed that when you've got oily hands it can be very difficult to wash off the oil? It is the different densities of the liquids which makes this happen. Similarly, it can be tricky to wash up an oily pan with water.

The waves occur when the bottle is moved from side to side because the rocking action means that energy moves through the liquid in the bottle, creating waves. In the real ocean waves occur in a similar way when the wind causes energy to move through the water. Lots of interesting wave and ocean facts can be found at this website: **oceanservice.noaa.gov/facts/wavesinocean.html**.

Big questions

Pause and think a moment about the energy in the waves of oceans and seas without human beings making it happen or being able to control it. Think of the way that people have always feared the power of the sea. What are the biggest waves you've seen? Think of the God who set all that energy in motion. How does that make you feel?

Storm in a jar/clouds in a jar

Ratings

MESS   DANGER   DIFFICULTY

Theme

Storms in our lives; factors and conditions that affect us

Equipment needed

Two identical jars (use a heat resistant glass such as Pyrex); cold water for one jar; boiling water for the other jar; red food colouring

Before you begin

This experiment involves very hot water so it is important that it is either done as a demonstration by an adult, or with close adult supervision.

Experimental method

Fill the two jars with water, one with cold water and one with boiling water. Then simultaneously add a few drops of red food colouring to each and watch what happens.

Big thinking

In which jar can you see a storm and clouds appearing? Why does one jar have a storm and not the other? The food colouring falls through the water as it is heavier than the water.

In the cold water, it collects at the bottom of the jar and then begins to spread through the water due to 'Brownian motion'. This is the small, random shaking of the water molecules that start to spread the particles of food colouring around. The colder the water, the less they shake and the more time it takes for the colouring to spread.

So, in the hot water jar, the water molecules are shaking faster. This would cause the colour to spread faster on its own, but it spreads faster still as some water which has cooled at the top begins to fall to the bottom, and patches of hotter water rise to the top. These are heat-driven 'convection currents' or 'turbulence', which cause the food colouring to spread out faster through the fluid and not collect at the bottom. The red dye colours the water moving in these convection currents. These currents are what give small fluffy clouds or big thunderstorms their bumpy edges.

Big questions

In the stormy jar we see clouds forming. How do clouds make you feel? Might you feel differently about clouds if you lived in a country with a different climate? The different writers of the books in the Bible used clouds to mean different things about God, and they are often full of meaning: watch out for them in the stories you read: be a cloud-spotter! Do clouds hide things or make it easier to see them? Will there be clouds in heaven, do you think?

In the Old Testament, there are also many examples of God's presence in the cloud (Exodus 16:10, 19:9, 34:5; Numbers 11:25). In the transfiguration (Luke 9:34–35), God's voice is heard from the cloud and there is a cloud present when Jesus ascends into heaven (Acts 1:9–11). Another important place where we see the imagery of clouds is when we hear of the second coming of Jesus, his coming in glory (Mark 13:26; Revelation 1:7).

Cartesian diver

Ratings

MESS 💡 DANGER 💡 DIFFICULTY 💡💡

Theme

Feeling under pressure; people in the Bible who felt under pressure

Equipment needed

A plastic bottle filled to the top with water; material to make a 'diver'

Before you begin

In this experiment you will need a 'diver'; there are a number of options as to how this diver can be made. A pen lid, without a hole in the top, with a small amount of play dough or plasticine is effective, as is a straw with plasticine over one end (see photo online). A small, sealed sachet of sauce would also make a good 'diver', and if you're feeling particularly creative you can actually make the figure of a diver with scuba equipment out of foil, a straw, a paperclip and play dough – go to this link for an example: **www.coolscienceexperimentshq.com/bottle-diver-science-experiment**.

Experimental method

Place the 'diver' in the top of the bottle of water and seal the lid; the 'diver' should float. Squeeze the sides of the bottle and watch the 'diver' sink (you might have to squeeze very hard). As you release the pressure on the bottle, the 'diver' will rise back up to the top of the bottle.

Big thinking

Why does the 'diver' sink? This experiment is about buoyancy force and density. The diver floats because the air trapped in is less dense than the water. So, while it is pulled down by gravity, the upward buoyancy force – equal to the weight of water the diver displaces – is greater, so it floats. As you squeeze the bottle, the pressure you exert is transferred to the water and compresses the bubble of air inside the diver, which gets smaller and becomes denser. Water also flows into the diver, and it becomes heavier than the weight of the water it displaces. So, gravity wins and the diver sinks!

See 'Moulded plasticine' (p. 30) for a further explanation of buoyancy forces.

Big questions

The Bible is very realistic about the ups and downs of life. Have you ever felt like the person who wrote Psalm 69:1–3?

> Save me, O God,
>   for the waters have come up to my neck.
> I sink in the miry depths,
>   where there is no foothold.
> I have come into the deep waters;
>   the floods engulf me.
> I am worn out calling for help;
>   my throat is parched.
> My eyes fail,
>   looking for my God.

Many of us feel there are times in life when we are sinking down and can't do anything to stop it. Our mood might go down, things might be going wrong for people around us, the global news seems to be all depressing – like the diver going down and down, the bubble of air inside us gets squeezed out. What helps you find your 'bubble of air' to rise up again? Can you see when other people are feeling 'squeezed'? How might you help them?

Refraction of light

Ratings

MESS 💡💡🔅🔅🔅   DANGER 💡🔅🔅🔅🔅   DIFFICULTY 💡🔅🔅🔅🔅

Theme

Perception

Equipment needed

A cup; a coin; water in a jug or bottle; gaffer tape

Before you begin

This is an experiment that is visually effective if it is done in pairs, with one person pouring the water and the other sitting in a position where they can watch the coin appear.

Experimental method

Place a coin in the bottom of a cup and place the cup at a distance where you can just no longer see the coin. Mark a spot to stand on the floor with gaffer tape if you have some over-eager participants. Start to fill the cup with water slowly (it may work best if someone else does this so you do not adjust your position), and as the water level rises you will begin to see the coin reappear, even though the coin is still at the bottom of the cup.

Big thinking

The coin disappears when you move it away because light only moves in straight lines. As it moves away, your line of sight is blocked by the side of the cup.

Why does the coin reappear? It is because of the refraction (bending) of light. There is much less refraction of light through the air but through water the refraction is considerably greater – this is because the molecules are closer together in the water than they are in air. Looking through the water, the coin is perceived to be much higher in the cup than it actually is – it even looks a bit as if it is floating!

Big questions

Have you ever been in a situation where you thought you knew what was happening but you didn't quite understand the whole truth? Like this experiment with refraction, where your eyes weren't showing you the whole truth? Paul writes about how now we know only in part, but then we will know fully, even as we are fully known (1 Corinthians 13:12).

If it takes a lot of effort to see the full picture, how does that make you feel about judging other people? About your side of an argument? About deciding what God is like?

Water rockets

Ratings

MESS 💡💡💡💡💡 DANGER 💡💡💡💡💡 DIFFICULTY 💡💡💡💡💡

Theme

God's power

Equipment needed

A two-litre plastic bottle half filled with water; a cork wide enough to plug the bottle; a pump with a needle long enough to go right through the cork (such as a football pump); a launcher made out of strong card or wood; a sheet of card

Before you begin

Find a safe, clear outdoor space to launch your rockets and make sure any younger children are supervised at a safe distance from the launch pad. When making the launcher, the material used must be very strong, strong enough to support the weight of a bottle half filled with water.

You should of course also retrieve your bottles after they have been launched.

Experimental method

Plug the bottle securely with the cork, turn the bottle upside down and place it carefully into the launcher stand. Use the sheet of card to made a cone shape to stick to the bottle to give it a rocket shape. Insert the needle of the pump through the cork into the water in the bottle (you may find that it is easier to make a small hole in the cork first to stop the needle getting blocked with broken cork). Begin pumping and the rocket will fly into the air!

Big thinking

Why does the rocket fly? As air is pumped into the bottle, air pressure inside the bottle will increase. This pushes on the water in the bottle. Water is an incompressible fluid – if you squeeze it, its volume does not change. So the increase in air pressure is transmitted through the water to the cork. After a while, when the pressure pushing down becomes too great, the cork will pop out of the bottle. The water is pushed out of the bottle, which causes the rocket to react in the opposite direction and fly into the air – and you will probably get wet! This is an example of Isaac Newton's Third Law of Motion which says that for every force, there is an equal and opposite reaction.

You can find a video demonstration at **www.science-sparks.com/2012/03/12/ making-a-bottle-rocket**.

Big questions

What helps your faith 'fly'? In other words, what would it take to make you feel like that rocket, soaring closer to Jesus, showering blessings on everyone around you? Do you feel held back? (If so, what's holding you back?) What 'pressure' would help you take off?

Moulded plasticine

Ratings

MESS 💡 🔲 🔲 🔲 🔲   DANGER 💡 🔲 🔲 🔲 🔲   DIFFICULTY 💡 💡 🔲 🔲 🔲

Theme

Being in the world but not of the world, not being shaped into the world's mould

Equipment needed

A large bowl of water; plasticine

Before you begin

For most effective results, make sure your two starting pieces of plasticine are very similar in size.

Experimental method

Take a small piece of plasticine and mould it into a shallow bowl. Place it into the bowl of water and watch it float. Now, take the plasticine and mould it into a ball shape. Ask people what will happen when they place it back in the bowl. Place it back in the bowl – does it behave as they thought it would? (It should sink this time.) Ask people if they can explain why the same weight of plasticine would both float and sink.

Big thinking

An object placed in a liquid has two forces acting on it: the force of gravity, pulling it downward trying to make it sink, and an upward buoyancy force in the liquid trying to keep it afloat.

Over 2,000 years ago, while having a bath, the Greek mathematician and inventor Archimedes realised that the buoyancy force was equal to the weight of water pushed aside by the object.

Plasticine has a density which is greater than water. So, when you roll it up in a ball, the weight of the ball is greater than the weight of water it pushes aside. The buoyancy force is less than the force of gravity pulling the ball down, so it sinks.

When you make the plasticine into a shallow bowl, the 'object' now includes a lot of air which is less dense than water. The weight of the object is lighter than the weight of the water it pushes aside when it is placed in the water, and the upward buoyancy force is larger than the pull of gravity, and so the plasticine floats.

This is how huge ships made of very dense iron float when, if they were crushed down into a block of iron, they would sink. Boats sink when they get a hole in them because water replaces the air and so the weight of water pushed aside is less that the whole weight of the boat and water that fills it.

Big questions

What shapes and moulds us? There are references in the Bible to being shaped and moulded using the analogy of the potter's clay (Jeremiah 18:3–4, Isaiah 64:8, Romans 9:19–21). Paul also speaks of being shaped when he talks of not being conformed to this world or moulded in its image (Romans 12:2). Can you think of a time when something on social media has shaped your views? Or when advertisements have? A teacher? Friends? Family? The Bible? Messy Church? A book or film? Would you say that experience helped you become more 'Jesus-shaped' or less?

Instant ice

Ratings

MESS 🔦 🔦 🔦 🔦 🔦   DANGER 🔦 🔦 🔦 🔦   DIFFICULTY 🔦 🔦 🔦 🔦

Theme

Being changed

Equipment needed

Two plastic bottles; filtered or deionised water; tap water; a freezer

Before you begin

This experiment needs plenty of preparation time and it's best to have a practice before you do it 'on the day'. It is best done as a demonstration, but if you have access to a large freezer and have plenty of time to prepare, this can also be done as an interactive activity.

You need the two different types of water as tap water will not 'supercool' in the same way as filtered or deionised water. Make sure there is room in your freezer for the two bottles to stand up and make sure you will be near the freezer for a couple of hours, as the bottles will need to be checked regularly.

Experimental method

Fill a bottle with deionised or filtered water and another bottle with tap water (you don't use the tap water in the experiment but it is just so you can gauge whether the other water is ready). Place both bottles in the freezer and check on them every 15 minutes or so (but do not touch them!). When the tap water freezes, which will take approximately 2–2½ hours, then the filtered water is ready to remove from the freezer – this should not be frozen yet.

There are now two options: hit the side of the bottle or tap it on a surface and watch the water instantly become ice, or alternatively pour out the water on to some ice in a bowl and watch it turn straight to ice, creating an ice tower.

Big thinking

Why doesn't the filtered water freeze at the same time as the tap water? Water usually freezes at 0°C but with filtered or deionised water it is possible to cool the water below the usual freezing point. This is referred to as 'supercooling'.

Why doesn't the water freeze at 0°C? Why does the water turn straight to ice when the bottle is jolted? When water freezes, molecules that are moving randomly in all directions in the liquid must come together into a semi-uniform pattern in a crystal lattice. To do this, it helps to have a template – such as a piece of dust, a rough surface or another ice crystal – to help the water molecules fit together. This is called nucleation. Very pure water does not have impurities to act as nucleation sites, so it cools below the usual freezing point. Tapping the bottle causes sound waves to move through the liquid, bringing water molecules together rapidly, which starts the freezing process. There are other complex and exciting supercooling experiments and a couple of these can be found at **www.bbc.co.uk/science/0/23065582**.

In clouds, there are often drops of supercooled water, especially when the air is moving rapidly upwards, as in a thunderstorm. This can be very dangerous for aircrafts. When a plane flies through supercooled water, the drops nucleate on the windscreen and wings of the aircraft. This makes it hard for the pilot to see, and can make the aircraft heavier as ice builds up on the wings. This in turn can make the plane difficult to fly, and has caused some air crashes in the past. Most large modern planes have heating systems in the wings to melt any ice that forms.

Big questions

In life, we sometimes get 'knocked' or 'jolted' like this bottle. It isn't always a pleasant experience! The Bible is full of people God wanted to do a special job for him who needed to change drastically before they could do the job: Saul's life was radically transformed when he met the risen Christ on the Damascus road; Moses, unsure of himself and lacking in confidence, encountered God and then led God's people from slavery to freedom in the promised land.

Knocks will come: can we trust that God has us safe in his hands and can we look for the way he's changing us for good through these difficult and sometimes shocking experiences?

Making music

Ratings

MESS 💡💡🔅🔅🔅 DANGER 💡🔅🔅🔅🔅 DIFFICULTY 💡🔅🔅🔅🔅

Theme

Offering our song of praise to God

Equipment needed

Jars (at least three or four of the same or a similar size); water; spoons; food colouring in a few different colours

Before you begin

Make sure your jars are the same or very similar in size and line them up ready to make your musical instrument.

Experimental method

Fill each jar with a different amount of cold water and make each a different colour with the food colouring. Gently tap each jar with a metal or wooden spoon and listen to the different sounds.

To make this a bit harder, you could talk about which jars make the lowest and highest sounds. Why is this? Do you think the food colouring might have made a difference to the note? Test this.

Big thinking

Why do the different jars make different sounds? The sounds you hear are caused by sound waves, which are themselves caused by the glass vibrating as you hit it. The frequency of sound depends on how fast the glass is vibrating. When a glass contains more water, the vibration is slower and the pitch is lower. Conversely, when the glass contains less water, the vibration is faster and the pitch is higher. If you're feeling particularly musical, try to work out how to fill the jars to create a musical scale or even a tune. The more jars you use, the more possibilities there are!

You could do this experiment a slightly different way with some plastic water bottles with different amounts of water in. Rather than hitting the bottles, blow over the top of them. Now what do you hear? Which has the highest and lowest pitch? It should be the opposite of what you found when you hit the jars. This is because in this case, it is the vibration of the air in the bottle and not the actual bottle that causes the sound you hear. In the bottle with only a little water in, there is a longer air column and the sound waves in the air vibrate slower so that the pitch of the note is slower. With a lot of water and little air, the sound waves in the air vibrate faster and the pitch is higher.

Big questions

The person who wrote one of the Psalms said, 'Let everything that has breath praise the Lord!' (Psalm 150:6). Sometimes we can praise God through words, but what do you think it means to praise God without words? Do non-humans praise God, do you think? Do trees and rivers? Do animals? How would you praise God silently? Is it possible?

Perspective

Alister McGrath is the Andreas Idreos Professor of Science and Religion at the University of Oxford. His most recent books include the award-winning *C.S. Lewis: A life* (Hodder & Stoughton, 2013) and *Enriching our Vision of Reality* (SPCK, 2016).

I was an atheist when I was a teenager. Why? The main reason was that I was studying science at school, and was convinced that science made it impossible for any thinking person to believe in God. Then I went to Oxford University to study science at a deeper level. I began with an undergraduate degree in chemistry, and then did doctoral research in the biological sciences. And that's when I discovered how wrong I was! I realised that Christianity made so much sense of our world, including explaining the successes and limits of science. It was as if somebody had turned a light on, and I saw things clearly for the first time. I began to read C.S. Lewis a few years after my conversion, and came across a quote which seemed to me to identify the really important issue here: 'I believe in Christianity as I believe that the sun has risen – not only because I see it, but because by it, I see everything else.' I found that exciting then – and I still find it exciting today!

So what did I discover? The first thing I realised was that atheism was much less interesting and convincing than I had thought! It left so many questions unanswered. I also came to see that Christianity could help me to make sense of science, and give me a bigger picture of reality than science ever could on its own. Science is wonderful in helping us to understand how the world works. But it doesn't tell us anything about why the world is here, or what our lives are all about. Science clarifies the mechanisms at work in our world – but we need to know what it means as well. I found the image of a 'big picture' very helpful here. Science fills in part of this picture – but only part. Faith fills in another important part of this picture. And together, they give us a deeper and richer understanding of ourselves and our world.

For example: science is very good at explaining how we came to be here. But it doesn't tell us *why* we are here. And for each of us, that's a very important question. What is life all about? What am I meant to be doing? Faith doesn't *deny* science. It *supplements* it. Faith enriches a scientific vision of reality. One of my favourite biblical texts to make this point is Psalm 19:1: 'The heavens declare the glory of the Lord.' It's a wonderful text. The scientist can tell us all about the nature of the stars, how old they are, and the vastness of the universe in which they are placed. But faith tells us that those stars are wonderful reminders and reassurances of the love of God for each of us (Psalm 8). The God who created those stars also created each of us – and we matter to him. That's one of the reasons why there are so many believing scientists; they realise that their faith enriches their science and sets it in a helpful context.

Now, there are times when faith needs to challenge science. But that happens when some scientists start thinking that science on its own can answer all our questions – which it can't. Over the years, I've had lots of interesting arguments with atheist scientists such as Richard Dawkins about the meaning of life and the role of science. Dawkins is a good scientist, and loves the beauty of the natural world as much as I do. But there's a big difference between us! Dawkins sees nature as complete in itself. But I see it as a signpost to the greater beauty of God. That means that I can appreciate the beauty of a glorious sunset, or the solemn stillness of a starlit night, while also seeing them as beautiful pointers to something still more wonderful. That helps me to appreciate nature all the more, while at the same time making me want to worship and praise God and, finally, to be in his presence.

My professional job is to teach students about science and faith at Oxford University. It's a wonderful job, and I love it. Many students still think of science and faith as being at war with each other. It's an idea that professional scholarship abandoned 25 years ago, but it still lingers in the media. Once people see how faith and science can enrich each other, they start to see things in a new way. I had that experience 40 years ago, and it's wonderful to see others doing the same today!

2

Earth, stars and space

Mavis Crispin comes from an atheist family, but became a Christian through the ministry of Dr Martyn Lloyd-Jones. She had an exciting career in teaching, specialising in primary-school science, enjoyed a happy marriage and brought up three sons. Now a widow, Mavis feels that God has led her into new things: theological training, work as a mission partner in Peru and Rwanda, and serving in ordained ministry in a parish in London.

Introduction

'When I consider your heavens, the work of your fingers, the moon and the stars which you have set in place, what is mankind that you are mindful of them, human beings that you care for them?' (Psalm 8:3–4)

Earth, stars and space – what a wonderful arena to investigate, learn and reflect on. Just as we are encouraged to study God's book of revelation (the Bible), we are also encouraged to study his book of nature. Both point to his glory and design, his wisdom and purposes. From 'Stardust' to 'Dinosaur hunt', this chapter embraces the theory of evolution, the Big Bang, the laws of motion, and biblical anthropology. Many of these are growth areas in science, but have sometimes been used negatively in our society to challenge and undermine biblical authority. I recommend the courses run by the Faraday Institute in Cambridge to learn from scientists who have thought this through and talk about it in a coherent and user-friendly way.

I have trialled these activities in a variety of contexts: the Diocesan Rural Schools in Butare (Rwanda), a self-styled Christmas roadshow with my own grandchildren (north-west England), a science cafe in my parish church (London) and children's summer clubs in shanty town churches in Lima (Peru). Although different cultures receive it differently, all have been excited and motivated. In Rwanda, the children had never seen dinosaur models; in Peru they knew more of the planets than their own land mass of South America. In the UK, where children are more used to a hands-on approach, they were hesitant to make biblical links.

In all places, it was gratifying to see the enthusiasm with which adults and children together engaged with this approach.

The writers of the books of the Bible were probably more aware of the earth and stars than we are, as they lived closer to the land and had no light pollution to stop them seeing the night sky. In the creation story of Genesis 1, the heavenly bodies' creation is firmly placed as late as day four, perhaps to avoid the perception that they were in any way gods themselves. Abraham was promised a family 'as numerous as… stars in the sky'. The mysterious planet earth with all its untameable forces was seen as created by God and in his control: 'The earth is the Lord's, and everything in it' (Psalm 24:1). Jesus was closely connected with the agricultural land of the Middle East and well acquainted with the wild forces of the sea. In Revelation we are told of the appearance of 'a new heaven and a new earth' (Revelation 21:1). Human beings belong to the planet they were born on even after its total redemption.

Stardust

Ratings

MESS 💡💡💡💡💡   DANGER 💡💡💡💡💡   DIFFICULTY 💡💡💡💡💡

Theme

Fine tuning; God creates elements for life

Equipment needed

A picture-based periodic table (easy to find online); objects (or photos of objects) made of different elements; dough; cocktail sticks/toothpicks

Before you begin

In this investigation we are learning about the chemical elements essential to life, and how they combine to make compounds. It is not necessary to stick with the elements made here or the objects made from them. Explain that we are making big models to represent very small particles.

Explain that the periodic table is used by scientists to categorise different elements. Those in the same columns of the table have similar properties.

Experimental method

Give out the objects that represent some essential elements on the periodic table. Distribute amongst the group, e.g. oxygen in a container, pencil with graphite (carbon), copper bracelet/wire, plant (nitrogen), an iron nail, silver coins/spoon, a magnet, a diamond/gold ring.

Ask people to try and identify the material the objects are made of, using the picture-based periodic table. Alternatively, pictures could be used. Ask people what these are made of. Can they be matched to the periodic table and its symbols?

Talk about how these elements can combine to make life-giving compounds e.g. water (H_2O) – two hydrogen atoms and one oxygen atom – or salt (NaCl) – one sodium and one chlorine atom. Make models of molecules by rolling dough into balls to represent different atoms. Connect with toothpicks (see photo online).

Big thinking

When the universe began at the Big Bang, only the lightest elements were made – hydrogen and helium. The essential elements for life were formed later in stars, strong nuclear forces holding particles together, enabling carbon, oxygen and iron to form. In fact, the way the universe is put together appears just right for this to happen and for life to emerge. For some, including Christians, this makes them think of how God is behind how the universe was made and works.

Everything on earth is made of elements, and all elements are made of atoms. Most things are made up of more than one element, which is what we have represented with our models. You might not have been aware that water is made up of two gases: hydrogen and oxygen. It's amazing that everything in our entire universe is ultimately made up of around 100 basic elements.

Big questions

We need certain elements to live, such as oxygen (which we breathe) and carbon (which makes up most of our bodies). These things will keep us alive, but truly to live full lives, Christians believe we also need God and the things he gives us.

We are 'connected' right at the most microscopic level of our bodies. Do you think it's fundamentally human to be connected at every level?

What can you not live without? What kinds of things do you think God gives us to help us live better?

The blue planet

Ratings

MESS 💡💡💡💡💡   DANGER 💡💡💡💡💡   DIFFICULTY 💡💡💡💡💡

Theme

The earth; God creates a unique planet for a unique people

Equipment needed

Dark sheet; sequins, glitter and shiny paper; one small blue 'earth'; one very large blue 'earth'; beans, buttons or little pieces of card; objects to represent what's gone wrong; glue; empty cups with writing on

Before you begin

This is a creative way of exploring the Big Bang and the unique adaptation of the earth to support life. It is possible to be flexible with some equipment; for example, you could use corks instead of cups.

Explain that the Big Bang is a plausible theory about how the universe may have started and does not undermine the biblical account.

Experimental method

Spread out a dark sheet with nothing on it. Let the group describe what they see. At a prearranged signal like a loud clap (you could even use something that explodes like a party popper), participants who are surrounding the sheet throw on handfuls of glitter, sequins, bits of shiny paper which scatter all over the sheet. There is one very small blue, special-looking planet in all this, on the far side of the bang. It looks insignificant and is hard to find but when someone does find it, swap it for a large equivalent planet, which is mainly blue (see photo online). We now focus on the blue planet earth. At this point the Genesis account of separating water and dry land could be read. Use beans, buttons or squares/hexagons of card to glue on rough outlines of land mass.

What sort of things belong on land mass? (Animals, people, buildings, rocks, etc.) Place pictures or photos of these things on the land. The Bible calls these things good and gives the responsibility of stewardship to humankind.

We read in Genesis that the rebellion of humankind led to disruption in behaviour and relationships. This has repercussions for the natural world and how it can be used and enjoyed. Present symbols, objects or pictures to represent this dysfunction (see photo online). Put cups with words over ones that human beings have impacted and what we might do about it. What is left? Think about natural disasters such as volcanoes and earthquakes. See 'Rock around' activity (p. 44).

Big thinking

Although the earth is very special, it is just a very small speck compared to the size of the universe! Today, scientists believe that the universe began with 'the Big Bang'. It is very hard to conceive the magnitude of force or the timescale of this. At the beginning, all the energy in the universe was crammed into a very, very small, very, very hot piece of space: a minute and a half after it was formed, it was 1 billion degrees centigrade hot! Over the past 14 billion years, it has expanded and cooled to make the vast and beautiful universe we see today.

Big questions

Although science helps us to understand how the universe has evolved and changed, the Bible says that God created the universe out of nothing; something beyond our understanding. In the account of Job 40, God speaks of things beyond understanding. But we can be amazed at what God's creation is. Take time to thank God for something in creation that you think is wonderful.

When James Irwin, an American astronaut, collected rock samples on the moon, he was distracted by the beauty and uniqueness of the earth floating in space. What made it so stunning? Talk about God giving humans beings stewardship of the earth's resources. How can we stop spoiling the earth and work towards its healing and renewal?

Rock around

Ratings

MESS 💡💡 DANGER 💡💡💡 DIFFICULTY 💡💡

Theme

Foundation of rock; material and spiritual significance

Equipment needed

A collection of rocks; things to scratch with (such as an iron nail); water tank; rulers; magnifying glass; vinegar with dropper; cone with bottle; bicarbonate of soda; protective cover

Before you begin

It takes time to put together a rock collection of sufficient variety. These could be borrowed from church members or a local school. Alternatively, small rock collections can be bought cheaply online.

The skills to investigate are common to all sciences. Make sure the group understands what is meant by observation, measurement and the importance of fair testing when, in this case, doing the scratch test.

Experimental method

Arrange or hide a collection of various contrasting rocks. If you have hidden them, get your group to find one each. Invite the group to observe, describe and measure the rocks. You could run a series of tests to find out about each rock's qualities. For example, test hardness by scratching with a fingernail and then with an iron nail. Test its acid resistance by dropping vinegar on to the rock with a dropper. Do the floating test – does it float in water? (Only volcanic rocks float.) Use a magnifying glass to look for fossils.

Put all the rocks together and listen to clues to identify each rock. For example, I am made of crystals that are white and sugary, and I fizz when acid is put on me (answer: marble). This activity depends on what types of rocks are in your collection (see photo online).

Big thinking

The earth is made up of rocks of all different types and different states. Some are very hard – like granite, which is made from the hot, molten rock that comes from some volcanoes deep within the earth. Others are very soft, such as chalk, which is made up of the compressed shells of sea creatures from long ago, or sandstone, which is layers of sand from the bottom of rivers and oceans squeezed together.

Rocks can also tell us something about the history of life on the earth. Fossils are imprints of long-dead animals that lived millions of years ago, like dinosaurs or small sea creatures. They remind us of how different the earth was in the past.

Did you know that not all planets are made of rock? Some, like Jupiter and Saturn, are called gas giants because they are just big balls of gas, mainly hydrogen and helium, without a solid surface. And some other small moons and planetoids are mainly made of ice.

Big questions

The word 'rock' is often used in the Bible. Many will be familiar with the parable of the rock and the sand. In the Hebrew scriptures (the Old Testament), God is sometimes described as a rock (Genesis 49:24, 1 Samuel 2:2). God is a firm place, a place of shelter, good for foundations. After Peter's confession of Christ, he is described as a rock on which the church is to be built (Matthew 16:13–18). What aspects of rocks that you have discovered today could also be used to describe God?

Some rocks are malleable and illustrative of how God shapes us, e.g. the potter and the clay (Isaiah 64:8, Romans 9:21). Rocks can change in other ways (e.g. heat up) and are subject to weathering, erosion and pressure. How do you think God might want to change you?

Some rocks are extremely valuable, like precious stones. Did you know that God sees you as more valuable than anything that can be found on earth?

Volcano

Ratings

MESS   DANGER   DIFFICULTY

Theme

Power of creation

Equipment needed

A small yogurt pot or similar; sand, slightly damp; cling film (optional); a plate or bowl; bicarbonate of soda; vinegar; red food colouring

Experimental method

Ask people what they think a volcano is. Explain that we are going to make a model of a volcano and watch it erupt!

Pile some sand on to the plate, and shape it into a cone. Then make a hole in the top of the pile, and place the small yoghurt pot (or similar) inside. If you cannot get one small enough, then line the hole with several layers of cling film to make the hole watertight.

Place some bicarbonate of soda into the pot or cling film. You can experiment with how much you need. Then, add some red food colouring and mix. Finally, add some vinegar and watch the lava flow down the mountain! (Note: See 'Bicarbonate fizz' on p. 215 – it uses the same reaction as here.)

Big thinking

The vinegar and bicarbonate of soda react together to make the gas carbon dioxide, which makes the mixture fizz and expand in volume, flowing out of the pot down the sides of the sand pile. It looks just like lava flowing down a volcano, but of course is not hot!

Lava comes from deep inside the earth where the rocks are not solid, but soft. Although rocks seem very hard, in fact the surface of the earth is constantly moving around, pushed by the motion of the hot rock inside the earth – a process called plate tectonics. The surface is divided into different 'plates' which rub against one another and cause earthquakes and volcanoes. In fact, although the lava in the experiment is not hot, it is similar to real lava in that it contains a lot of gas. This makes lava in a volcano rise to the surface as, with all the gas in it, it is lighter than the surrounding rock. Volcanoes put a lot of carbon dioxide into the atmosphere, which helps keep the earth warm enough for life.

There are volcanoes on other planets in the solar system, too. Mars has the biggest extinct volcano – Olympus Mons, which is 22 km high, three times the height of Mount Everest, the tallest mountain on earth. And not all volcanoes produce molten rock. On Jupiter's moon Io, there are some volcanoes of sulphur, which makes its surface bright yellow and orange. And the moon Triton, which orbits Neptune, has volcanoes made of nitrogen ice!

Big questions

Why do you think God's world contains volcanoes? What good might come of a volcano? How do you think he wants human beings to respond to volcanoes and the way they change life for the people in their regions? How might a seismologist's work be part of the kingdom of heaven, do you think? If you were creating a planet, would you include volcanoes? Why (not)?

Sometimes the emotion 'anger' can feel like a volcanic explosion. Have you ever experienced this yourself or been on the receiving end of an eruption of anger? What do you think is a good way of dealing with that sort of anger?

Sometimes 'joy' can feel like an eruption too. When did you last feel joy erupting and overflowing in your life? Some people say the Holy Spirit gives them this sort of joy when they are worshipping God: maybe you could try a few different worship styles to find which one helps you come closest to God. Some people come closest to God in loud music, some in quiet music, some in silence, some in Holy Communion, some in the outside world, some in learning something new or helping other people… or many other different ways: find out what makes joy bubble up in you!

Day and night

Ratings

MESS 💡💡💡💡💡 DANGER 💡💡💡💡💡 DIFFICULTY 💡💡💡💡💡

Theme

God is light, but darkness can be useful

Equipment needed

Polystyrene balls (10–12 cm in diameter); cocktail sticks, cut in half; felt-tip pens; light source

Before you begin

Explain that the length of the day – 24 hours – is the time it takes the earth to make one rotation, while the length of the year – 365.25 days – is how long it takes the earth to orbit the sun. Explain that other planets have longer days and years than we do. For example, the planet Mars' days are about the same as the earth's, but it takes two earth years to go around the sun.

The one-yearly orbit and 24-hour rotation of earth impacts life and how we measure time. You might want to find a short YouTube video on day and night, or rotation and orbit, to show before you get started.

Experimental method

Explain that the polystyrene ball represents the earth. Get people to stick one of the half-cocktail sticks in the top of the ball, and another in the bottom. These represent the north and south poles. Explain that the earth rotates every 24 hours around an axis joining these two points. You might want to mark the equator on the ball using a pen.

Stick some more cocktail sticks into the ball on a line that runs from the north to the south pole – one at the equator, others near the north and south poles. These represent people who live in different places. If you have time, you could invite people to draw the continents on the ball – have a globe available for people to copy.

Shine a strong light on to the globe e.g. lamp, projector or powerful torch (do not look into the light!) centred on the equator, so that the whole of one side is illuminated evenly. Line up the cocktail sticks with the boundary between the light and dark side of the ball. This is the moment people move into the sun's light as the earth rotates. Rotate the ball counter-clockwise and see when the cocktail sticks go into shadow – this is sunset. Do they go into the shade at the same time?

Explain that the earth's rotation axis is not straight up, but tilts a little. Tilt the north pole of the ball towards the light a little, so that the cocktail stick near the north pole is always in the light when you rotate the ball around its axis. This is what happens in summer hemisphere – it points towards the sun as the earth moves around its orbit and the days are longer. What is it like at the south pole? It should be always in the shade. This is what happens in winter hemisphere – it is pointing away from the sun.

Big thinking

The world experiences both light and darkness through each day, and different amounts of each as we go through the year, along with seasonal changes in temperature. Many plants and animals have adapted to this pattern. Some flowers open up in sunlight, and then close again at night. Some trees grow leaves in the spring and summer, and shed them in the dark days of the winter. Is darkness always bad?

Animals too are affected by different light levels and the seasons. Some hibernate in the dark, cold days of winter when there is not much food – ask people if they can think of any (squirrels, bears). You could have pictures of plants/animals and explain how light and dark affect them.

Plants and animals are affected when the amount of light changes – even humans. Because of the short days in winter, some people feel sad. When the clocks are changed in the spring and autumn, people's sleep patterns can be disrupted too for a week or so.

Big questions

Light and darkness are common themes in the Bible. Christ claims to be the light of the world (John 8:12); Christians are encouraged to be lights in this world; the first phrase God says in the Bible is, 'Let there be light', and it is described as good. Darkness, on the other hand, often represents evil. Light is coupled with truth and salvation (Psalm 27:1, Psalm 43:3) and revelation (Luke 2:32). In the book of Revelation, natural light seems not to feature in the new earth, as God is its light. Day and night are linked with laws of motion, rotation of the earth on its axis and elliptical orbits. God is described not only as creator but sustainer of the physical universe (Colossians 1:17). What do you praise God for about light? What do you praise him for about darkness?

There is light and dark inside all of us. What can you ask God for today that will enable your light to shine more strongly?

Spoon science

Ratings

MESS   DANGER   DIFFICULTY

Theme

Human beings

Equipment needed

A set of commemorative spoons (maybe from a charity shop); warm water in a bowl; magnets; a light source; a magnifying glass

Before you begin

Make sure the spoons are similar in size and equally shiny. You could discuss what kind of questions would be asked when we handle an unknown object and the value of using every sense.

Experimental method

Each person in the group needs a commemorative spoon of similar size, but with different crests or figures at the top (or one could be shared between two). Tell everyone to imagine they are aliens coming to earth and discovering these artefacts but they don't know what they are for, where they came from or who made them.

Invite them to investigate their object to find out what they can.

- Does it float or sink? Drop it into a bowl of water and see.
- Is it magnetic?
- Does it conduct heat? The safest way to do this is to put it into some warm water for a few minutes. When it comes out, is it warmer than when it went in?
- What happens when it's dropped? Try dropping it on to various different surfaces (carpet, wooden flooring, etc.).
- Are all the objects the same? Or are there differences?
- Does it reflect light? Hold it up to a light source and have a look. What can you see in the concave/convex end of it?
- Look closely using a magnifying glass. What do you notice?

Big thinking

(Remember you are aliens.) What did you find out about materials and their properties by tests and observations? What is the same and what is different? You might have discovered what properties they have, but our investigations cannot tell us 'who' made the spoons and 'why' they were made. Where do you think we could get that information?

We can learn a lot about the world and ourselves from science. But it deals with the 'what' and the 'how' questions we ask about the world. What is something made of? How does that thing happen? It cannot answer the 'why' questions that come up in our lives. That is the kind of question that philosophy, theology and religion seek answers for. Perhaps working together we get a bigger picture of the world and universe?

Big questions

Science tells us that the universe is wonderful and beautiful. That might make us think about how its creator values it and appreciates its beauty.

Science also shows us that the world is a place of order. Scientists have discovered the rules and laws that describe the way it works, which appear to be the same on the earth as they are in the most distant galaxy! This too might tell us something about the one who made it – that he likes things to follow a set pattern.

And the laws and rules that scientists have discovered seem just right for life like us to form – which might make people think about the purpose God had in making the universe and how special we are. But science only deals with the material the universe is made of. It cannot tell us what God is fully like. Only God showing himself could do that. We know why spoons were made. Why do you think God created human beings? Do you think he was just lonely, and wanted some friends? Or do you think he had a bigger purpose than that? How could we find these things out?

The Bible speaks of God loving what he has made (Psalm 119:64). It shows his qualities (Romans 1:20). All things are created by and for Christ (Colossians 1:16). The inverse, distorted image on the concave side of the spoon could generate a discussion about what has happened to the image of God in human beings.

Solar system

Ratings

MESS   DANGER   DIFFICULTY

Theme

The heavens declare the glory of God

Equipment needed

Eight cut-out discs of card in different sizes (see table below), one set per person; pictures of the planets of the solar system (from the internet); wooden rod (optional); cotton or string (optional); pens or paints (optional)

Before you begin

The planets are very different from each other; some are made of rock (terrestrial) and others are huge balls of gas (gas giants). The time taken to orbit the sun varies enormously, as do their atmospheres.

Experimental method

Explain that you are going to make a model of the solar system. First, give out a set of discs to every person. These represent the eight planets of the solar system. Some are small; some are big!

Tell people what the names of the planets are: Mercury, Venus, Earth, Mars, Jupiter, Saturn, Uranus and Neptune. Explain that the cards are all cut to scale and show the different sizes of the planets. Ask people to decide which disc represents each planet – put then in size order from smallest to biggest. When everyone is done, tell them the answer (see table below – the scale of the discs is 1 cm to about 5,000 km).

Next, ask them to place the planets in order from the sun. When they have all had a go, tell them the right answer – Mercury, Venus, Earth, Mars, Jupiter, Saturn, Uranus, Neptune. You can remember the sequence through the rhyme: 'Many Vulgar Earthlings Munch Jam Sandwiches Under Newspapers'.

Planet	Size of disc (1 cm = 5,000 km)	Distance from sun 10 cm = 30 million km
Mercury	1 cm	10 cm
Venus	2.5 cm	40 cm
Earth	2.6 cm	53 cm
Mars	1.5 cm	82 cm
Jupiter	30 cm	3 m
Saturn	25 cm	5 m
Uranus	10 cm	10 m
Neptune	10 cm	16 m

Show some pictures of the planets – either projected on to a screen or printed out. There are lots you can download on the internet – try the NASA site, for example. You could get people to colour in their discs so they look like the planets.

Now, try to make a model of the solar system. You will need a large space – about 25 m long; you can scale the distances to fit the space you have. With the sun at one wall, using the distances in the table, get people to stand at the orbital distance of the planet. Here, 10 cm represents about 30 million km!

Optional: Using the wooden rod and cotton, you could make a mobile of the solar system.

Big thinking

The earth and other planets all move around the sun. Because they are all different distances (and sizes), they look very different from earth. Some of them are just gas – ask which ones (Jupiter, Saturn, Uranus and Neptune). Some are extremely hot (Mercury, because it is close to the sun, and Venus, because it has a very thin atmosphere). None, as far as we know, apart from the earth, can support life, although recent observations of Saturn's moon Enceladus suggest the ocean under its icy surface might be a good place to look!

The planets are so far away that they appear as only points of light in the sky. Over 500 years ago, people thought that the earth did not move and the planets and the sun went around the earth. But, as people got better at observing the night sky, and invented telescopes, which meant we could take a closer look, they realised that the earth was a planet like all the rest and that all of them went around the sun. This is an example of how scientific facts change through time as observations improve.

Over the past 50 years, we have learned a lot more about the planets by sending space probes to them. These show how varied and beautiful each one is. And they have changed the facts of what we know about planets. For example, the planet Mars changes colour as it orbits the sun, which some thought was a sign of plants growing as the seasons changed. But when the first space probes reached Mars in the 1950s, they found it was covered in craters, like the moon, and was very dusty, although there are some features on the surface that look like dried-up rivers. Might it have had more water in the past?

The earth may be small, but it is the only planet where human beings are able to live. This is because it has the right temperatures and weather patterns to allow plants to grow, among many other things. Be amazed at the uniqueness of the earth for supporting life!

Big questions

There are numerous verses in the Bible (e.g. Psalm 93:1) which speak of the earth not being moved; in the past, people believed this literally. What do you think it means, now that we know the earth is moving around the sun all the time?

Pleiades

Ratings

MESS 🔦🔦🔦🔦   DANGER 🔦🔦🔦   DIFFICULTY 🔦🔦🔦

Theme

Infinite God

Equipment needed

Maps of different constellations (find online); black paper; pins; light source

Before you begin

You might find it helpful to learn about the night sky using an app such as QContinuum (**www.qcontinuum.org/planets**).

Experimental method

Give people some maps of different constellations. Choose some well-known ones that can be seen in the night sky from your locations. In the northern hemisphere, Ursa Major, Orion, Cassiopeia, Cygnus, Andromeda and Gemini are some examples.

From these maps, use a pin to prick out constellations on to black paper. Shine a bright light through to see it on a wall or the ceiling – you may need to darken the room to do this. You could use an OHP or video projector that produces white light if you have one. Explain that the names of the constellations are very old and go back to ancient times when people thought they could see animals and the images of gods in the stars. Ask people to look at the constellations and suggest names for the patterns they can see. Then share with them the names of the constellations and the images people thought they could see.

You could invite people to make up their own constellations using pin holes in cards and project them, giving their own names and stories – perhaps even ones from the Bible!

Big thinking

Stars are huge balls of very hot gas in which nuclear reactions turn hydrogen – the lightest element – into helium and other heavier elements, releasing energy in the process. The sun is our nearest star. The next one, Promina Centauri, is over four light years away, which means that light takes four years to travel from there to the earth. It only takes eight minutes from the sun!

There are all different sizes of stars. Some are smaller than the sun. The smallest known one is called OGLE-TR-122b – a red dwarf that is only slightly bigger than the planet Jupiter, the largest planet in our solar system. The biggest star that has been found is VY Canis Majoris, a red hypergiant. Nearly 5,000 light years from earth, it is 2,000 times bigger than our star!

The sun is vital to life on earth. All of the energy we have comes from the sun. It gives us light and warmth, and plants use its light to make energy through photosynthesis. Without the sun, life would not be possible on earth. Our sun is 5 billion years old and, in another 5 billion years' time, when it starts to run out of hydrogen in its centre to make energy, it will grow into a red giant star, and expand outwards to fill the inner part of the solar system… swallowing Mercury, Venus, Mars and the earth!

Big questions

Some of the names of the constellations we use are found in the Bible – for example, 'Can you bind the beauty of the Pleiades?' (Job 38:31). The Pleiades is an open star cluster in the constellation of Taurus, only about 444.2 light years away – that means it takes over 400 years for the light from these stars to travel to earth!

Stars play an important role in the story of the birth of Jesus. The wise men or magi were ancient observers of the night sky and, in Matthew 2:9, were guided by a star to where Jesus was born.

The Bible's attitude to stars is that they are God's work and they glorify him (Nehemiah 9:6, Isaiah 40:26). The Jews were forbidden to worship stars (Deuteronomy 4:19) and they are used by Paul as a metaphor for Christians in this world (Philippians 2:15).

When you look up at the stars, you can thank God for his amazing creation. What else do you see regularly that reminds you of the wonder of God's creation?

The lesser light

Ratings

MESS DANGER DIFFICULTY

Theme

Seek and know the light; be a light

Equipment needed

A light source; a range of surfaces to test; play dough or rocks and wet plaster

Before you begin

We will be exploring the difference between reflections, shadows and direct sources of light.

It's worth making a chart depicting the phases of the moon (you can find plenty of these online, or make your own by doing a nightly observation of the moon over a month). This can be shown as a horizontal series of diagrams or presented as a circle or made large on the floor for a game of hopscotch. A flick book is another interesting way of learning the phases of the moon.

Experimental method

The moon reflects 12 per cent of the light from the sun that hits its surface. It seems brighter at times according to its orbit around the earth. Shine a light on to a range of surfaces. You could use a collection of different rocks and grade their brightness. Remember to keep the conditions the same, e.g. level of darkness, intensity of light and size of surface.

Without an atmosphere, water or life, the moon is very battered and covered in craters where rocks have landed on it. Build your own model of the surface of the moon: you could use play dough, or drop rocks on to wet plaster.

Big thinking

The moon is the earth's only natural satellite. It is thought to have formed when a small planet collided with the earth and material thrown off collected together. There are different types of landscape on the moon. The dark 'seas' were once thought to be oceans, but now we know they are barren volcanic plains. In between, the landscape is covered with craters. In fact, we only see one side of the moon, as the length of its day is the same as the time it takes to orbit the earth, so the same face always points at the earth. We had never seen the far side of the moon until space probes were sent. It is different from the side we see, being very heavily cratered without any volcanic plains.

As our natural satellite, the moon is easily observed and admired. It is the only other body in the solar system that humans have visited. We benefit from its effects in a number of ways. The moon's gravitational pull governs the oceans' tides, impacting the natural world. Less well known, but still important, it helps to stabilise the rotation of the earth on its axis. Without the moon, the axis of the earth would wobble around, making the seasons more extreme!

Big questions

Genesis calls the moon the 'lesser light'. It is referred to elsewhere in the Bible to mark when festivals start (Nehemiah 10:33), as a reminder of God's splendour (Job 31:26) and as sign of end times (Acts 2:20). The moon cannot shine by itself; it just reflects the light of other objects (such as the sun). Christians need to be exposed to the light of Christ in order to reflect it into dark places. How can we best do this?

Talk about how God provides protection through light.

Always moving and all ways moving

Ratings

MESS 💡💡💡💡   DANGER 💡💡💡💡   DIFFICULTY 💡💡💡💡

Theme

Action; reaction

Equipment needed

Marbles; various objects to drop (e.g. plasticine); toy vehicles; fabric; paper (e.g. sandpaper)

Before you begin

We are going to explore gravity in different ways. Fair testing and measurement are important. For example, you must drop the marble from the same level; you must give the pendulum the same force each time, i.e. let go of it as opposed to giving it a push.

Experimental method

Drop marbles of different sizes from the same height. Do they reach the floor at the same time? Drop a variety of objects from equal height; you could use plasticine, changing its shape for each drop. Why do you think they do or don't always reach the floor at the same time?

Line up toy vehicles. Let them run down a slope and vary the surface of the slope, e.g. with different fabrics or papers. Observe and record the difference friction makes.

Big thinking

The scientist Galileo discovered that under the action of gravity, all objects fall at the same rate – on earth about 10 metres per second squared. All the objects you dropped should have hit the floor at the same time. But the presence of air can slow some things down. One of the astronauts who went to the moon, where there is no air, dropped a hammer and a feather and they hit the ground at the same time – watch the video at **www.youtube. com/watch?v=KDp1tiUsZw8**. You might want to try it out yourself – but here on earth, air resistance will slow the feather down and it will land after the hammer!

It's the same with the cars going down the slope. Gravity pulls down at the same rate, but the friction of the different surfaces slows them down at different rates.

Gravity is the force that pull objects together. Isaac Newton (1642–1727), one of the greatest scientists of all time, discovered a law describing how gravity works, and used it to describe the motion of the planets in the solar system. The strength of gravity a planet has depends upon its mass. The moon has only one-sixth of the gravity that the earth has, which is why people can't walk normally there.

Some people get confused when they see astronauts floating weightless in space and think there is no gravity in space. But there is gravity everywhere! When you stand on the surface of the earth, gravity is pulling you down. It is pulling down the surface of the earth too, but the rocks of the earth are strong enough to resist this pull and stay still, stopping you moving down. If you were going around the earth in a spaceship, even standing on its wall, you are still being pulled down by gravity. But so is the wall of the spaceship. So as you are both being pulled down by gravity are the same rate, it feels like you have no weight. It's like going over the top of a rollercoaster. You and the car are falling at the same rate, and just for a moment you feel weightless – and have a funny feeling in your tummy too!

Big questions
If there are laws built into the way the whole universe functions, do you think there are laws built into the way all human beings in all countries in all times of history function?

Perspective

Tim Middleton studied natural sciences at Cambridge and is now a PhD student at Oxford working on earthquakes.

My love of science began in the mountains. When I was a child my family regularly went on holiday to Switzerland. We would rent a chalet for two weeks of the summer and spend our time walking in the Alps. The lower slopes would be covered with coniferous forest and grassy meadows, whilst the skyline would be filled with breathtaking views of rocky crags and snowy peaks. I was always desperate to get to the top and, once I was old enough, I would race ahead to ensure that I was the first to take in the summit view. Looking back at these memories, it was here that I first developed a passion for the outdoors and an interest in how natural landscapes are shaped.

However, it was in a rubbish dump by the side of a Greek motorway that I decided to pursue geology in earnest. I was a third-year university student and I was standing in a heap of broken furniture and rotting vegetables looking up at a 50-metre-high cliff. The cliff itself was perfectly smooth, almost glassy, and soft to touch. If you looked very carefully you could just make out some long lines that ran up the rock face. What I was looking at, it turned out, was a series of around 50 fossilised earthquakes. Whenever a quake took place, individual mineral grains would be ripped apart and immediately polished flat again to create the perfectly even surface in front of me. The lines were giant scratches that showed the direction of movement: in each event the cliff had gone upwards and the ground I was standing on had gone down. In fact, over millions of years it is earthquakes like these that build the world's mountain ranges; this was how the beautiful scenery of the Alps had been made. Seeing first-hand the sheer power that went into shaping the earth's landscape was phenomenal and I knew that I wanted to find out more.

Now, as a research scientist, I have spent the last four years studying earthquakes in northern China. I use satellite images, as well as trips to the field, to piece together the remaining clues about historic and prehistoric earthquakes. How big were they? How often did they happen in the past? And what should we expect from future events in the same place? One of the earthquakes I have been studying, which took place in 1739, broke part of the Great Wall of China and has left a clear scarp that runs across the landscape. I got to visit this scarp a couple of years ago, and the extent of the upheaval caused by this single event is astonishing. You can stand at one end of the fault and see a line that runs into the distance for nearly a hundred kilometres. Back in the laboratory, I estimated that the energy involved was equivalent to more than 7,000,000,000 sticks of dynamite.

But there is a bittersweet edge to all of this. The earthquakes that create the stunning beauty of the natural world around us are also responsible for great devastation. For example, the 1739 earthquake is thought to have killed 50,000 people. This is not easy to deal with. For me, this prompts thoughts about the brokenness of the world we live in. I have always been a Christian – I grew up going to church – and the God I have grown to know is a caring God. But how can a caring God be squared with such terrible loss of human life?

What I have found is that the science I have studied has led me to a deeper and more serious exploration of my faith. This search often produces more questions than answers, but it was my curiosity about the natural world that sparked my curiosity about the nature of God. Furthermore, although complete solutions are hard to come by, science is able to help us with part of the answer. By mapping fault lines and studying previous earthquakes, we can say approximately where and roughly how often shocks are likely to take place in the future. This in turn enables communities to prepare and, hopefully, some lives to be saved. Science opens a window on to our messy world. And one thing that does seem very clear to me is that this is exactly how a caring God would want us to be using our science.

3
Air

Chris Hudson works full-time for The Bible Reading Fellowship, leading Barnabas RE Days in primary schools, training teachers and writing material for the Barnabas in Schools website (barnabasinschools. org.uk). An experienced teacher, he has authored over 20 books for schools, and blogs at **www. glitteringdelights.blogspot.co.uk**.

Introduction

Air provides a rich symbolism for understanding God's world, because it is vital for life – but also invisible. Our whole earth is surrounded by a very thin layer of breathable atmosphere (including nitrogen, oxygen and carbon dioxide gas), so as a general introduction, take a model globe and a piece of paper. Ask volunteers to indicate with the paper just how far out they *think* this layer of air extends. Then lay the paper flat on the globe. *That* represents just how thin the layer actually is – a few miles. It also explains why breathing gets harder at the top of a high mountain! The natural movements of our atmosphere (wind) are also used to describe the power of God's Holy Spirit.

For experiments and demonstrations requiring the effect of the wind, have a powerful electric fan (and an extension lead) available as back-ups, for when the weather outside doesn't oblige, or when a wind-driven idea needs testing out. If you do take people outside, always ensure that the route and outside space are suitably safe.

Stories from the Bible that feature air, wind or breath include the creation story in Genesis 1, the wind in the story of Noah drying up the land, the wind that dried up the Red Sea when the Hebrew people had crossed it, the wind in Elijah and the still small voice, Ezekiel's vision of dry bones, Jesus calming the storm, Pentecost and the Holy Spirit.

Invisible air pressure

Ratings

MESS ⚛⚛⚛⚛⚛   DANGER ⚛⚛⚛⚛⚛   DIFFICULTY ⚛⚛⚛⚛⚛

Theme

Christians believe that God is invisible – but that doesn't mean he isn't there

Equipment needed

Paddling pool or large tray; plastic jug; water; fairly rigid plastic cups; waterproof card; lots of spare towels

Before you begin

If you can't find any waterproof card, you can make your own by covering ordinary card in sticky tape. It's best to do this activity while standing in a paddling pool, but if you have older children, a large tray works just as well.

Experimental method

Explain that you are going to demonstrate a strange effect. Take a plastic cup half-full of water, then hold a watertight piece of card to cover the top. Turn it over, still holding the card on the cup… and then take your hand away. The card should remain there, holding in the water. Discuss what might be happening here.

Set people the challenge of trying this out for themselves with different types of card and cup – are some better than others, and why? Toddlers and infants will be especially fascinated by this phenomenon – and, by the end, probably extremely wet.

Big thinking

Explain that air pressure is an invisible force pushing into all of us, and that it is pushing up into the card with greater force than the mass of the water being pulled down by gravity. (Without the air pressure, our bodies would explode – which is why space explorers wear pressurised suits.) The card provides the air with something rigid to push against. Without it, the water drops.

Big questions

How can we know if something is there, when we can't see it?

Air pressure is invisible until we see it in action. Similarly, God is invisible, but he still changes people's lives every day. Jesus came to show us what God was like, as a human being. God is much more than a 'force' – he cares deeply about us.

Bible links include: Paul's speech in Athens (Acts 17:23), John 1:18, John 5:37, Colossians 1:15.

Air resistance and asking questions

Ratings

MESS  DANGER DIFFICULTY

Theme

Truth, curiosity, resistance

Equipment needed

Safe higher surface to stand on (chair, small stepladder); lots of scrap A4 sheets of paper

Experimental method

Show two identical pieces of paper. Explain that we're going to drop them both down on the ground at the same time. Which one will hit the ground first, and why? (Expect a range of answers.) Then screw up one of the pieces into a tight ball. When it comes to dropping the two pieces, hold the unscrewed-up sheet horizontally. Now which one will hit the ground first? (Expect answers talking about 'the heaviest', but point out there is the same amount of paper in the ball as before.)

When you drop both pieces, the 'ball' will hit the ground first. Why? Is it 'heavier'? No, but the 'stretched-out' shape encountered more air resistance on the way down, rather like an open parachute. The ball fell faster, not because it was heavier, but because it had a smaller surface for the air to push back on.

Optional: Cheat! Throw the ball down. (Is that fair? Why not?) Hold the flat piece of paper vertically before dropping it. (Does that make a difference? Why?)

Try different ways of shaping and dropping the sheets of paper to make them fall more slowly, and faster. Compare them by dropping two at a time, using both hands to make the drop simultaneous. Which shapes are the slowest and fastest at falling? Why?

Optional: See who can make the slowest/fastest shapes, then have a knock-out competition.

Big thinking

The science of making things travel through the air in different ways is called aerodynamics.

Establishing truly 'fair tests' is the backbone of all experimental science, but sometimes it is very hard to achieve. Other variables can affect the results, including the experimenter's own desire to prove their own theory right!

Big questions

How 'aerodynamic' do you feel you are? In other words, what is there in your life at the moment that's like the air, stopping you getting where you want to be? What is there in the life of your church or school or workplace that is meeting resistance, stopping you moving in a good direction? How might things need to be reshaped, like those pieces of paper, to help you be what you want to be, or go where you want to go? What part might Jesus play in that reshaping?

Candle flames and invisible gases

Ratings

MESS   DANGER **DEMO ONLY**   DIFFICULTY

Theme

Dependence on God through the Holy Spirit

Equipment needed

A table with a top 75–100 cm off the floor; candle on a solid base/candleholder; large glass container or beaker with an airtight lid; matches or lighter; tapers

Before you begin

Place a small lit candle on a surface. Ask: what does a lit candle need to keep burning?

Experimental method

Either cover the candle with a large glass container, or place it in a large glass container and cover the top. Ask: what do we think is going to happen?

Invite your audience to notice if the flame is changing shape or colour.

Allow the flame to 'die'. Then, just as it goes out, remove the cover – and the extinguished flame should relight (the wick and surrounding gases should be hot enough to ignite the fresh oxygen). Could we estimate how long it will take for the flame to go out – then test it?

Alternatively, quickly place a burning taper near a wick that's just been snuffed... and see the candle reignite (the heat ignites the gaseous fuel). Some of your audience might experiment with this (safely), or possibly repeat the other demonstrations if appropriate. What do we notice?

Big thinking

'Combustion' (or burning) is a high-temperature chemical reaction between a fuel (e.g. wax) and an 'oxidant' (usually oxygen gas), that produces light and heat. Michael Faraday was a Victorian scientist (and devout Christian) who created a series of popular Christmas lectures called 'The Chemical History of the Candle'. They include many more practical demonstrations and useful ideas for Messy Church activities!

Big questions

How are we like that flame? Do you feel your faith is more like a burning flame or a smouldering wick? Who is there in this room whose faith is like a brightly burning flame? Why not ask them what fuels their flame – you might be surprised!

A burning flame needs a steady supply of fuel (just as we need food) and (invisible) oxygen gas (just as we need to breathe). Christians believe we need to have God's Holy Spirit working inside us, to live life to the full. In the Bible, the two saddened disciples who met Jesus on the road to Emmaus described their 'hearts burning within us' after meeting him again (Luke 24:32). The coming of the Holy Spirit in Acts 2:4 is also described like a mighty refreshing wind. See also Jeremiah 10:23 and 2 Corinthians 3:5.

Candle flames and convection currents

Ratings

MESS   DANGER **DEMO ONLY** DIFFICULTY

Theme

Faith; the Bible; the Holy Spirit

Equipment needed

A table with a top 75–100 cm off the floor; large candle on a solid base/
candleholder; matches or lighter; tin foil or card cut/shaped to make a windmill
or spiral; cotton or wire; computer projector and white screen/wall; a book

Before you begin

Ensure your demonstration 'works' beforehand – it can be remarkably fiddly!

Experimental method

Light the candle. When the flame is burning well, release a little piece of light
tin foil above it. See it rise a little, then fall. Discuss what might be happening.
(Gases are rising and lifting the tin foil.)

Show a simple tin foil or thick card windmill or spiral, either suspended on cotton
(easier) or balanced on a wire (fixed in a stable position). Can you make it turn?
(This takes a lot of practice to get right, but looks very effective when it does work!)

Place the candle on a surface near (but not in) the beam of a computer projector,
with a white screen or wall behind. Ask: can you see the hot gases rising from
the flame? (No.) Slide the candle into the light beam, and show the shadows
of the convection currents of warm air rising from the candle. If you hold a
book at a safe distance above the candle, the flow is visibly disrupted. Some
of your audience might experiment with this (safely), or possibly repeat the
other demonstrations if appropriate. What do we notice? Why can we see this
happening on the screen, but not when we look at the candle itself? (The path
of the light waves from the projector is being bent by rising gases on their way
from the projector to the screen, creating moving shadows.)

Big thinking

Rising warm air can create shadows and other visual distortions such as the mirages seen along roads on a hot day. (When we were using the projector, the light was refracted by the different densities of hot and cold air – which means it didn't have a straight path to the screen.) This is also why movements of air in the earth's atmosphere make the stars in the night sky appear to 'twinkle' – because out in space, they definitely don't!

Big questions

How can we put our trust in a God that we cannot see? The author of Hebrews 11:1 said, 'Faith is the substance of things hoped for, the evidence of things not seen' (KJV). The Christian faith provides us with ways to understand both ourselves and our world. (A scientist might call this a 'working hypothesis'.) For Christians and others, the words of the Bible and God's Holy Spirit are like the light of that computer projector, revealing hidden forces at work. This is why Christians meet to read the Bible, to pray and discuss together what God might be saying to them through its pages – because it helps make sense of everything (Psalm 119:105, John 16:13).

Paper planes: ailerons and rudders

Ratings

MESS   DANGER   DIFFICULTY

Theme

Holy Spirit; guidance and decisions; the tongue

Equipment needed

Scrap A4 paper; adequate space (such as a corridor); upturned box or wastepaper basket

Before you begin

If you have younger children, you might want to have some pre-made paper planes that they can simply add the aileron or rudder to.

Experimental method

Demonstrate how to make a simple paper plane from one sheet of A4 paper. Ask: can you make a paper plane that will fly around a corner into a target (upturned box)?

Show how its direction of flight can be affected by creating an aileron (flap, see photo online) or rudder. Set the challenge of making a plane that consistently flies around a corner into a target area.

Big thinking

Real aircraft usually feature a hinged vertical rudder on the fuselage and hinged horizontal ailerons on the wings, all of which can be adjusted by the pilot to create smooth turns. These produce 'drag' (air resistance) that disrupts the passage of air along one side of the plane, causing it to turn. Of course, the size of the fin and the angle with which it is bent will all have an effect. They're comparatively small, but work similarly to the rudder on a ship, shaping the air flow and turning the craft… providing it keeps moving forward! (Why don't they work if the craft is stationary?)

Big questions

A little change can make a big difference! Small changes to a rudder have a serious impact on a plane's flight – and apparently small human decisions can have a big effect, depending on the different forces at work around them. There are many Bible stories that hinge on a moment's decision or the impact of a few words (e.g. Naaman the Syrian in 2 Kings 5 or David sparing Saul's life in 1 Samuel 24). The letter of James (3:1–12) memorably likened the power of the human tongue to the effect of a tiny rudder on a large ship. Do you feel 'small' or 'large'? How much of a difference do you feel you can make?

Acoustics: air conducting sound

Ratings

MESS DANGER  DIFFICULTY

Theme

Listening to God

Equipment needed

Ticking clockwork watch or kitchen timer; plastic/wooden rulers or other lengths of similar material; long length of garden hose; cardboard; scissors; sticky tape

Optional: two tin cans/plastic cups; drill; a long bit of string; nails/dowelling

Before you begin

This activity might require two people, to supervise both the testing area and the construction area.

Experimental method

Everyone in your group shuts their eyes for a moment. How many different sounds can they hear? Provide a range of rulers (or similar), challenging people to hear a ticking object by placing one end to their ear and the other on the object. Notice how this changes the sound.

Experiment outside with home-made megaphones and ear trumpets (made from cardboard and sticky tape), so we can either direct sounds more powerfully in one direction, or hear them more clearly. (Do some megaphone/trumpet shapes work better than others? Why?) A long garden hose also conveys sound a long way!

Optional: The classic 'two-tin-cans-or-plastic-cups-and-long-bit-of-string-pulled-tight' experiment is another illustration of sound travelling through another material. If using tin cans, ensure the surfaces are clean, smooth and safe. Pierce the can/cup's base using a drill, attach the string by inserting an end through each hole, loop it around a short nail/piece of dowelling in the base, pull it out of the hole again and then knot it.

Big thinking

'Sound' is a wave of vibrations travelling through the air to reach our ears. That's why, if we go swimming, everything sounds different if we listen under the water – because the vibrations are travelling through a fluid, and that changes the quality of the sound. In the vacuum of space, everything is silent!

Big questions

How do we listen to God? How can we hear God speaking to us? When Jesus taught the Sermon on the Mount to a large crowd (Matthew 5), that doesn't mean he was standing on the top. The valley beside that mountain is a natural amphitheatre – so if a large number of people sat down, they would be able to hear a single speaker facing them *from below*. His use of a moored boat (Luke 5:3) possibly also made use of the surrounding harbour's acoustic qualities.

How does God speak to you? At different times in the Bible, God spoke through the weather (1 Kings 19:12), angel messengers (Luke 1:26), dreams (Matthew 1:20), hearing or reading scripture (Luke 4:21), other people (Exodus 18:13–27), music (2 Chronicles 20:21), prayer (Romans 8:26–27)… but the way we listen can affect what we hear, so it's worth trying to listen *in more than one way*!

Air resistance: Cayley cones and parachutes

Ratings

MESS ♛♛♛   DANGER ♛♛   DIFFICULTY ♛♛♛♛

Theme

God's protection; courage

Equipment needed

Safe higher surface to stand on (chair, small stepladder); large pieces of paper; stencils (plates) of different sized circles for drawing around; scissors; sticky tape; toy model parachutist figure (optional)

Before you begin

This activity might require two people, to supervise both the testing area and the construction area.

Experimental method

Demonstrate how a simple piece of paper (held out flat horizontally, then released) falls to the ground: in a series of side-to-side motions. Ask: why doesn't it fall straight down? (Answer: air resistance, pushing up against it.)

Show how to make a 'Cayley cone' by cutting out paper discs of different sizes, cutting a slit from the centre to the edge, pulling the two cut edges together, slightly overlapping them, and fixing the shape of the cone with sticky tape. Ask: using this method, can you make a cone that will fall as slowly as possible?

Try to make three Cayley cones of different sizes using the same type of paper. Ask before testing: which do we think will fall slowest? Why?

Test this hypothesis. What's going on?

Big thinking

Bizarrely, it's the bigger ones that fall slowest, because they encounter greater air resistance on their larger surfaces. We cannot 'see' this force until we test it out. Parachutes use air resistance to make a controlled descent possible, protecting many lives as a result – but that doesn't make it any easier for someone about to take their first jump!

Sir George Cayley pioneered early experiments into air resistance, lift and flight by making simple paper cones and measuring how fast they fell to the ground. This led to further experiments with gliders.

Big questions

Parachutes have protected and saved thousands of lives in danger. What helps us to feel safe when life gets scary? In dangerous times, many Christians have spoken of feeling surrounded by God's protection, especially when travelling. It's a constant theme in the Old Testament (e.g. Deuteronomy 31:6; Joshua 1:6, 23:6; 2 Samuel 10:12; 1 Chronicles 22:13, 28:20).

Wind, seed dispersal and autogyros

Ratings

MESS    DANGER   DIFFICULTY

Theme

Seeds as symbols of God's kingdom; sharing the good news

Equipment needed

Safe higher surface to stand on (chair, small stepladder, etc.); examples of seeds that use air resistance to scatter themselves in the wind; thin card or thick paper; paperclips; scissors; rulers; pens/pencils

Before you begin

This activity might require two people, to supervise both the testing area and the construction area.

Have a few 10 cm x 7.5 cm rectangles of card/paper cut out and ready to use. Depending on the age and ability of your experimenters, these pieces could have the folding/cutting areas already marked on – or not. (See photo online.)

Experimental method

Demonstrate a few real-life examples of wind-driven seed dispersal.

Show a working design of a rotating autogyro-style 'dropper' (see photo online). Set the task of creating an autogyro that will take as long as possible to hit the ground. Cut and fold the card, apply a weight (paperclips) to the central strut, then fold out the flaps. Test, then make adjustments to weight and flaps. (The higher the distance of the drop, the easier it is to see how well your autogyro performs.)

Which designs work best? Find the 'winning' (slowest) autogyro by staging a knock-out contest in which one person holds two autogyros as high as possible before dropping them simultaneously.

Big thinking

Many plants use the wind to disperse their small seeds as far as possible, using a variety of methods (e.g. dandelions, sycamores). The bigger the seed, the larger the wind-catching 'flaps' need to be. Modern powered autogyros use a similar technique – they might look like helicopters, but the rotating vanes have no power source apart from wind resistance. They're basically a rotating kite that uses a horizontal rotor to push them forward.

Big questions

In Mark 4:1–20, Jesus likened the kingdom of God to a farmer scattering seed far and wide. (How could the wind make that job easier or harder?) The first Christians often found themselves scattered across the Roman Empire by hardship or persecution – but this led to the good news of Jesus being taken as far as Africa (Acts 8:26–40, noting how Philip is driven by a whirlwind), Malta (Acts 28, again after a storm) and beyond!

How could suffering be turned into something that helps other people? Could God use a difficult thing in our lives to make a better thing happen for someone else – like sharing the good news of Jesus with them?

Measuring our breathing

Ratings

MESS   DANGER   DIFFICULTY

Theme

God giving us life; the importance of the Bible

Equipment needed

Peak expiratory flow meter (many people own one); a large bowl containing water, with a jug; plastic bottle (at least 2.0 l) with appropriate marks on the side to show capacity (use a measuring jug to work out the capacity, marking out 0, 0.5 l, 1.0 l, 1.5 l and 2.0 l, starting from the base of the bottle, using a waterproof pen); long flexible plastic tube; antiseptic wipes; display chart where scores can be recorded

Before you begin

This activity might get quite competitive; be aware of people who might overstretch their ability to breathe.

Ask: how much breath do you have in your body? If you were to breathe out, how big a breath would it be?

Experimental method

Show and demonstrate two ways of measuring how big your breath is:

1 Use the peak expiratory flow meter, which measures the force of that breath. Record and display your own 'score'.
2 Create a capacity meter, using one breath to fill a submerged bottle with expelled air. Before each measurement is taken, the bottle must be first filled with water, then quickly inverted in the bowl so that it doesn't empty. One end of the tube then needs to be placed underneath and inside the bottle's neck. Using the measurements you marked on the side of the bottle, work out how much air you can breathe out in one breath.

Emphasise and show the use of antiseptic wipes and their importance to ensure no spreading of germs through mouthpieces.

Ask: might adults or children have the greatest peak flow or lung capacity – and why? Using the equipment, find out:

1   how much breath you can expel in one go ('peak flow'). Who has the highest 'peak flow' at Messy Church today?

2   which person in the room has the greatest lung capacity, using the bottle and tube apparatus. Take a deep breath… and blow slowly once into the tube.

Big thinking

Our lungs transfer oxygen into our blood circulation system, which moves it around the body and then expels the unwanted carbon dioxide. Don't be surprised if most adults completely fill your bottle with expelled air – the average male lung capacity is about six litres!

Breathing is synonymous with being alive, which is why first aiders check for it first when examining accident victims. Many people with breathing problems need to have their peak flow and capacity regularly measured, but regular exercise often improves this – especially swimming.

Big questions

What gives us life? Genesis 2:7 describes how God 'breathed' life into the first human being. Ezekiel's vision of the valley of dry bones (Ezekiel 37:5) and Paul's speech (Acts 17:25) similarly trace the origins of life to the breath of God. However, in 2 Timothy 3:16, Paul declares that the very words of the Bible are also crucial for a full life, saying that 'all Scripture is God-breathed and is useful for teaching, rebuking, correcting and training in righteousness'.

If physical life depends on air, how true do you think it is that our spiritual life depends on the breath or word of God?

Measuring wind direction

Ratings

MESS   DANGER   DIFFICULTY

Theme

Holy Spirit; Pentecost; Easter story; fear of others' opinions

Equipment needed

Home-made 'compass rose' of durable heavy materials that can be used to show compass directions outside your venue; long thin pieces of cloth or newspaper; large electric fan and extension lead; pole (possibly made of bamboo cane); magnetic compass; craft materials and suitable stencil for the shape; wire or dowelling; pen-top

Before you begin

Note: are you near a traditional parish church, sporting a wind vane featuring a rooster? If so, could you incorporate this into your demonstration?

This activity requires two people, to supervise both the testing area and the construction area.

Ask: which sorts of people might need to know what the wind is doing today? (e.g. Sailors? Fishermen? Pilots?) How can wind direction affect the weather? (Depending on where it's coming from, that'll affect its temperature and humidity.)

Experimental method

Show your compass rose, establishing with your magnetic compass where north is. Set the challenges:

1 (easy) Find out which direction the wind is coming from, using a long piece of cloth/newspaper pinned to a vertical pole.

   Stand the pole at the centre of the compass rose, and use the movement of the cloth/newspaper to work out from which direction the wind is currently blowing.

2 (tougher) Quickly make a wind vane that will balance on the pole and turn to face the direction the wind is coming from.

Construct a weather vane by creating a shape that will swivel on the top of a vertical thick piece of wire or thin piece of wooden or plastic dowelling. (See photo online.) Fix your design to the pen-top, slot that on to the wire, then try it out. If it doesn't perform well, add a few extra 'tail feathers' to increase the drag, or adjust the position of the pen-top, away from the 'tail'.

Finished? Decorate your wind vane with patterns, or an appropriate Bible verse!

Big thinking

A wind vane shows where the wind is coming from and where it is going to. Understanding 'the way the wind is blowing' has long been important for farmers, sailors and anyone else dependent on the changing weather.

Big questions

How could God's Holy Spirit be like the wind – and how might we be like this wind vane? Jesus spoke of the unpredictability of the Holy Spirit in John 3:8. The coming of the Holy Spirit at Pentecost empowered the disciples in ways beyond their wildest imaginings. Would you prefer God's Spirit to be predictable and always the same, or like a wild wind? Why do you think you feel that?

However, public opinion can be just as unpredictable! The story of Simon Peter's denial of Jesus during his trial (Matthew 26:73–75) features a rooster crowing, which is why many churches feature one swivelling on a weather vane. It's a warning to Christians not to betray Jesus as Simon Peter did, by fearing the changing opinions of others.

Alternatively, not heeding 'the way the wind is blowing' is an image of foolish behaviour and even ignoring God. In Acts 27, Paul's hazardous sea voyage to Rome was imperilled by his captors' complete disregard for seasonal wind conditions and sensible advice.

Perspective

Naomi Brehm is studying Physics at Durham. She loves worshipping Jesus, being creative and getting lost in nature.

Last year, a good friend asked me, 'How can you be a Christian *and* study science?' You may be thinking the same, but it seemed like such a strange question to me. I study creation *because* I love the creator! Science gives us the amazing opportunity to discover more about the world God has made.

'So God created human beings in his own image' in Genesis 1:27 (NLT), and that means we've been given something of his character, including intelligence and creativity. Our heavenly Father has given us brains to understand and engage with the world around us, and it glorifies him when we use that gift. He doesn't tell us to stop using our intellect when we come to church, or to turn off any logical thought processes when we pray. We don't have to decide between science and faith, like my friend believed. Rational thinking and relationship with God go hand in hand when you believe in an intelligent God who blesses us with a little fraction of that intelligence.

Secondly, he has made us to be creative. Science is often seen as a tough discipline that produces factual answers. Although it can be rigorous and challenging, to find those answers we can enjoy asking questions, exploring and researching. When I was about seven, I loved climbing trees, making mud pies and playing with insects in the school field. I still love being surrounded by natural beauty, getting muddy and exploring new forests and fields, and I think that's where science starts. As a child of God with a commission to be creative, I choose to pursue science as a joyful exploration of my environment, asking curious questions about the natural world and letting a genuine passion and interest be the driving force of my study and research.

Being a Christian in science means I can use the intelligence and creativity God has given me to understand the world he has made. It is a joy to learn new things about my creator each day, and a privilege to study his creation. In fact, I've found that studying physics *enhances* my faith and increases my love for Jesus. I'm fascinated by the strange behaviour of tiny particles in the quantum world, but how much more fascinating is the servant king? I love the logical problem-solving nature of mechanics, but how much more logical is the mighty Father's plan to save us? I see beauty in many physical phenomena and the maths that explains them, but how much more beautiful is the Spirit of truth? I'm in awe of the sheer scope of scientific study, but if our universe is huge, how much bigger is the one who created it?

In Matthew 7:7, Jesus says, 'Ask and it will be given to you; seek and you will find; knock and the door will be opened to you.' So let's keep asking about our world, keep seeking answers for the big questions of science and faith, and keep knocking on God's door to see what he wants to teach us along the way. There is so much still to discover in science, and infinitely more to learn about God, so why not start today?

4
Light and colour

 **Neil Hunt** CPhys MInstP is a chartered physicist who has worked in industry for over 25 years. A registered STEM ambassador, he has been involved in taking science and engineering activities into local schools, such as the Institute of Physics 'Lab in a Lorry' or robotic workshops. More widely, he supports STEM involvement through the Social Mobility Foundations eMentoring Scheme. He has been a Methodist local preacher, and is currently involved in his church in all-age worship and Messy Church engineering activities. He is married to Yvonne and has two boys.

Introduction

> God is light and in him there is no darkness at all.
> 1 JOHN 1:5 (NRSV)

Light and colour are all around us. We can produce all the light we need at the flick of a switch. When John wrote this verse, light would have been a much more precious commodity. If our sources of light have moved on from an oil lamp to an ultra-bright LED (Light Emitting Diode), does this change what we think it means that God is light?

I would like to recommend two books as background reading for this chapter. The non-scientist (and scientist needing to know how to explain things simply) should start with Dr Chris Ferrie's *Optics for Babies* (CreateSpace, 2013) with its elegant explanation of how rainbows are produced. At completely the opposite end of the spectrum, for those wanting something more thought-provoking is the excellent *Electromagnetism and the Sacred* by Lawrence W. Fagg (Continuum, 1999). Professor Fagg gives careful and considered thought to whether our modern understanding of light as electromagnetic radiation allows us to know more about God.

Some general points: experiments with light often work better in a darkened room; you can always build a makeshift tent from a thick blanket. Do warn people not to stare into bright lights, especially if you are in an otherwise darkened room, as their pupils will be wider.

Bible stories about light and colour include the creation story in Genesis, the rainbow in Noah's ark, the pillar of fire in Exodus, Joseph's coat of many colours, the different-coloured stones and cloths in the building of the temple, many references in the Psalms and in Job, Jesus describing himself as the light of the world and John describing him in those terms in John 1, the light of the world in Matthew 4, Jesus' transfiguration, the lamp on a stand in Luke 11, the bright light that Saul saw on the road to Damascus, the many uses of 'light' in the epistles, the rainbow around the throne of God in Revelation, the light of God providing all the light needed (Revelation 21) and, in the same book, the different-coloured stones in the city of God.

Light and shadow

Ratings

MESS 💡💡💡💡💡   DANGER 💡💡💡💡💡   DIFFICULTY 💡💡💡💡💡

Theme

'God is light; in him there is no darkness at all' (1 John 1:5); light and darkness: shadow and gloom or brilliance and sparkle?

Equipment needed

A light (a big or bright lamp or torch); thick cardboard in which to make holes; bulldog clip or blu-tack to stand the cardboard up; a box or cover for your light so you can control where it shines; a white piece of paper to act as a screen; a length of string

Before you begin

The science in this activity is a little basic but is fundamental to starting to think about how light behaves. Ask people what they know about light.

Experimental method

First, take three squares of card of the same size and make a small hole in the centre of all three. Make the hole just large enough to thread a piece of string or wool through (see photos online). With the light at one end, get people to arrange the pieces of card so that they can see the light through them. How do the pieces of card need to be arranged and what does this tell us about how light behaves? (The piece of string can be used to align the holes perfectly.)

Next, arrange the light to shine through a small hole (a 'point source') on to the white paper. Place a circle of card in between and examine the shadow ('umbra') produced. Now let the light shine through a larger hole (an 'extended source'). Note how the shadow has changed. The total shadow ('umbra') will be surrounded by a partial shadow ('penumbra').

There is now scope for the artier ones to make shadow puppets.

Big thinking

On one level, we can think of light travelling in rays – beams of light. A ray is the direction of the path taken by light. The sharp edge of a shadow reinforces that light travels in straight lines. The bigger the light, the more difficult it is to get a complete shadow. The bigger the light, the more likely there is a ray path from it to the observer. Think of the sun during an eclipse. This first experiment demonstrates quite clearly that light travels in straight lines and does not go around corners. However, 'Young's double slit experiment' (see p. 109) will show that light does not go in straight lines and does go around corners. The question 'What is light?' is quite a tricky one to answer.

Big questions

'God is light': what does that mean to you? What sort of light is he most like, from all the lights you can think of? Spiritually, God is the biggest light there is! John says that in him there is no darkness at all. What darkness can survive his glory? Some more questions could be: what does it mean to live in the light of God? How does God's light get into our lives? What things block us from living in God's light? Think about partial and full shadows… John, in his letters, tells us some ways to know we are living in darkness.

Spectroscope

Ratings

MESS   DANGER   DIFFICULTY

Theme

Taking a closer look; working out what something truly is

Equipment needed

Diffraction grating sheet/slides (available to buy online); cardboard tubes; scissors; sticky tape; thick, matt black paper; sharp cutting instruments (a fresh scalpel is ideal)

Before you begin

This activity builds a scientific instrument to explore how white light is made up of all the different colours. Ask people what other scientific instruments they know about. Everything from a simple magnifying glass through microscopes and telescopes helps us to see the world in more detail. Watch out for the clever ones that know about the Large Hadron Collider at CERN and that it is looking for the Higgs Boson.

To get this to work well it does need to be built with a degree of care and precision that some people may find frustrating. Obviously, consider carefully who in your Messy Church is safe to handle a scalpel.

There is some trial and error in getting the construction of the spectroscope correct so, in the true spirit of scientific endeavour, persevere.

Experimental method

(See photos online.) Each person will need to cut themselves a short length of cardboard tube. (We found about 4–5 cm to be a good length but yours may be different.) Line the inside of the tube with the matt black paper.

Cut two circles of the black paper slightly larger than the diameter of the tube. These will become the end caps. In one circle cut a long thin slit (shorter than the diameter of the tube) and the other a rectangular viewing window. Fix the disc with the slit to one end of the tube, folding it over so that light cannot get in around the edges, and then do the same with the other disc at the other end.

Cut a piece of the diffraction grating sheet just larger than the viewing window. Try not to get finger marks on the sheet! You now need to align the diffraction grating with the slit; the difficulty being that the lines on the diffraction grating are microscopically small and you cannot see them. Hold the slit up to a bright light and rotate the diffraction grating – when you can see a rainbow, you have them aligned. Tape the diffraction grating into place.

You can now use the spectroscope to investigate the different colours given off by different lights. An incandescent bulb will have a full spectrum; you may be able to see that energy-saving and LED bulbs have some colours missing.

Big thinking

White light contains a spectrum of colours: red, orange, yellow, green, blue, indigo and violet. It does not matter how many times you use the spectroscope to study a light source, the colours will always appear in this order. Depending on the lamp, you may have some colours missing, but never in the wrong order. James Clerk Maxwell (1831–79) showed that not only are the colours of light arranged in a spectrum, but that the light we see with our eyes is electromagnetic radiation. The electromagnetic spectrum contains everything from radio waves and microwaves through to both the light that you can see and the light you can't, to X-rays and gamma rays.

Big questions

What are the tools we use to study our faith? Chatting, discussion, prayer, books, Bible reading, confession (in some traditions). Holding ourselves up to examination is a hard thing to do. Being honest with ourselves that God already knows who we truly are, and still loves us, is just as hard.

Red sky at night

Ratings

MESS 💡💡💡 DANGER 💡 DIFFICULTY 💡

Theme

Lord of heaven and earth; creation and sustainment; care for the earth

Equipment needed

A tall clear glass or vase, the taller the better; water; Dettol or a similar disinfectant; a bright light

Before you begin

The colour of the sky is a thing of beauty. An interesting opening discussion is to ask everyone at the start how/why they think the sky colour changes.

Experimental method

This experiment demonstrates the effect of different colours of light scattering in the atmosphere.

Fill the glass with water and shine the light up through the base. Note whether it is white light all the way up. Add some Dettol to the water (how much is trial and error), and swill or stir a few times to mix the Dettol evenly. The water will now look cloudy. Shine the light up through the base again and note whether there is any colour difference up the glass.

When you get the amount of Dettol correct, you should be able to see that close to the bottom the light has a bluer tinge and that it becomes progressively more red the higher up the glass you go. (See photos online.)

Big thinking

Ask: what is up in the sky? There are any number of correct answers, from clouds to aeroplanes. See if anyone thinks of dust! Dust and other microscopic particles in the atmosphere *scatter* the light from the sun. When the sun is directly overhead it has a shorter journey to the ground. In the evening (and morning), the sun's light has a longer journey through our atmosphere and there is more opportunity for scattering. Blue light and red light behave differently. The shorter-wavelength blue light is scattered more than the longer-wavelength red light, so more red light reaches you on the ground.

Big questions

How fragile is the balance between light and dark on our planet? Just think that the light from the sun travels approximately 93,000,000 miles through space to reach us, but it is the air in the last 100 miles or so that changes what we see! The atmosphere also protects us from even shorter wavelengths and more harmful electromagnetic radiation. You could discuss why we need to wear sunscreen during the middle of the day. (The sun being directly overhead has the shortest distance through the atmosphere. The atmosphere has less opportunity to protect us as there is a shorter distance in which to scatter the harmful ultraviolet light.) There is an opportunity to discuss our part in the stewardship of the world. Within living memory, we have banned the use of CFCs (chlorofluorocarbons) to protect the ozone layer of our atmosphere. We are currently concerned about greenhouse gases. Care for God's creation is an important part of our discipleship.

Chromatography: colour splitting

Ratings

MESS ▼▼ ▼ ▼ ▼   DANGER ▼ ▼ ▼ ▼ ▼   DIFFICULTY ▼ ▼ ▼ ▼ ▼

Theme

Parts making up the whole

Equipment needed

Coffee filter paper, preferably white; glasses of water; either a collection of coloured felt-tip pens or brightly coloured sweets, e.g. Skittles or Smarties

Before you begin

This is an experiment that can take a long time to work so is a good candidate for starting at the beginning of your Messy Church session and returning to later.

The colours we see are often very carefully created. Pick up some paint charts from the local DIY store, and see that a paint cannot just be blue, but must be 'moonlit lagoon'. You could ask people whether they have a favourite colour. But more interesting would be if they are fussy: do they like all reds or just that particular shade between burgundy and claret?

This experiment has been run as part of a forensic analysis activity, in which a message is written, and people are challenged to work out with which pen it was written.

Experimental method

If using sweets: Cut a disc of filter paper, which sits on top of the glass with a tab that drops down into the water (see photos online). Place the sweet at the top of the tab and wait for the water to soak up the paper.

If using pens: Cut long thin strips of filter paper. Using felt-tip pens, colour a line about a quarter of the way up the strip and suspend it with the bottom of the paper (but not the pen mark) in the water (see photos online). Wait for the water to soak up the paper.

This will take around 5–10 minutes. Be careful not to leave it for too long or the colours cannot be separately identified. In both cases, the colour will be dissolved into the water, but the different colourings within the dyes will separate out and be transported different distances. Note how many different colours make up the original colour.

Big thinking

Science has developed many different techniques to determine what a substance is made from. It is particularly important in police forensics to know that paint is made up from different individual dyes. A paint sample left at the scene of a crime can tell them the exact make and model of car used for the getaway. Every paint mix has its own unique chemical 'fingerprint'.

This experiment works because the different molecules of the different dyes mixed to make the original colour are different sizes. The difference in size means that they are carried different distances by the water.

Big questions

Who makes up the unique mix that is your Messy Church? Can you identify each person's contribution – big or small? The Bible has a lot to say about being the people of God but perhaps think about what Paul says in his letter to the Corinthians about the church being the body of Christ (1 Corinthians 12:12–31).

Paint mixing: light combining

Ratings

MESS 💡💡💡💡   DANGER 💡💡💡💡💡   DIFFICULTY 💡💡💡💡💡

Theme

Rainbows – from Noah to Revelation

Equipment needed

Paint or felt-tip pens in the three primary (red, blue, green) and three secondary colours (cyan, magenta, yellow); paper; paint brushes; thick white card; pencils

Before you begin

The rainbow is one of the most iconic symbols from the Old Testament, and yet, curiously, the story in Genesis makes no mention of colour. This activity investigates how the whole spectrum of colours can be made from just three.

Do people know the primary colours?

The *primary* colours are red, green and blue. From these, the *secondary* colours can be made: cyan (blue and green), magenta (red and blue) and yellow (red and green). With one of these three sets of colour, all other colour can be produced.

Experimental method

If you have younger children, give them some paint and challenge them to paint a complete rainbow in the correct order. (Hint: you could use the mnemonic 'Richard Of York Gave Battle In Vain' to remember the correct order.)

Most people will be familiar with the brown sludgy colour that you get if you mix all the colours together. Get them instead to cut out a disc of card, divide it into segments and paint or colour them the six different primary and secondary colours. Push a pencil through the centre to turn it into a spinning top. Ask people what colour they think they will see when they spin the disc. The colours should blend to appear white.

Big thinking

When you mix all the colours of the paint together, you will get a brown muddy-coloured paint. But when you mix different colours of light together, something different happens. Ask: why do the paints appear different colours?

White light is made up of all different colours of light – the different colours of the paint help you see this. The chemicals that make up the paint reflect all different colours of light. When you shine white light, red paint will reflect red light, but will absorb the other colours. Green paint will reflect green light, blue paint blue light and so on. When the disc is spun, it rotates so fast that your eye and brain cannot recognise the individual colours and they all merge together to make it look white. This is demonstrating 'colour mixing by addition'.

Mixing paints of different colours behaves differently. A yellow paint is likely made up of pigments which reflect red, yellow and green light but absorb blue light. Blue paint is likely made of pigments which reflect blue and green light but absorb red and yellow. When you mix the two colours together, red, blue and yellow light are absorbed and the only colour that is left reflected is green. This is called 'colour mixing by subtraction'.

A rainbow forms because the drops of water act like a prism and split up the white light from the sun into the different colours your eyes can see. By the way, the human eye can see 10 million different colours!

Big questions

Rainbows! What are they to you – do you simply enjoy the science of them? Do you think it's okay to feel 'awe and wonder'? The rainbow appears to Noah as the sign of God's covenant (Genesis 9:13). It reminded Ezekiel of the glory of the Lord (Ezekiel 1:28). In Revelation, it reappears to remind us that, when God comes in holiness with his righteous judgement, he will remember mercy. What do rainbows mean to you?

In the Bible, one writer asks God to 'wash me, and I shall be whiter than snow' (Psalm 51:7) – asking God to forgive the mistakes that have messed up his life and to give him a fresh start. Think about the difference between mixing all the paint together – into a muddy brown – and how the colours merge to form white on the spinner. How might we need to ask God to forgive us and help us to make a fresh start?

Acids and alkalis: colour indication

Ratings

MESS 🔆🔆🔆🔆🔆   DANGER 🔆🔆🔆   DIFFICULTY 🔆

Theme

Colour in the Bible

Equipment needed

A large red cabbage; coffee (white) filter paper; acids you can find around the house, e.g. vinegar, lemons, pickled onions, cola, different fruit juices, ketchup; alkalis you can find around the house, e.g. bleach, toothpaste, soap, bicarbonate of soda, indigestion medicine; neutral substances, e.g. distilled water or tap water

Before you begin

Within the Bible, the word 'colour' occurs very rarely. (The NIV has 'colour', 'coloured' and 'colourful' in only eight verses.) Individual colours are mentioned a lot but usually to tell us something significant about a place or object. In science, colour is often used to indicate important facts about different substances.

The danger rating does depend on which chemicals you choose to test. Remember that you can always add water; dilute substances are less harmful than concentrated ones. It may change what colour you get, but you should still get a nice reaction. Safety glasses and gloves are always a good idea.

Litmus paper or universal indicator, which you may remember from school, is very cheap and readily available online. But it is much messier to make your own indicator paper!

Experimental method

Roughly chop the red cabbage and bring to the boil in a pan of water. Simmer for 20 minutes or so until the colour comes out of the cabbage into the water. There is a chemical called anthocyanin in the cabbage which will react to acidic and alkali solutions. Allow to cool before using it. Soak a coffee filter in cabbage juice and put aside to dry. (Everything up to this point could be prepared in advance.)

Cut the indicator paper into strips and test the substances that you have gathered by dipping the paper in your different substances. From the colour change you should be able to group the items into acids and alkalis (see photos online). Neutral things will not change the paper from a purple colour; acidic things will turn it red; and alkali things will turn it green/yellow.

Big thinking

The acidity or alkalinity of a solution is measured on the pH scale which generally goes from 1 to 14. pH stands for the power of hydrogen and is a measure of the number of hydrogen ions (H+) in the solution available to react with other substances. A solution of a strong acid, such as hydrochloric acid, will typically have a pH of around 1 or 2 as lots of H+ ions are released. Bleach or sodium hydroxide is a strong alkali with a typical pH of 12 or 13. Instead of releasing H+ ions it releases hydroxide ions (OH-) which neutralise any H+ ions. Water (pure) is neutral or pH 7. This is because the water molecule neatly splits into one H+ ion and one OH- ion which then proceed to balance each other out.

The colour of the indicator paper tells us how reactive the solution is. Testing water does not change the colour as it is neutral. If you tested fruit juices or fizzy drinks, were people surprised by how acidic they are? Did the experiment give them a greater appreciation of why dentists tell us to drink water?

Big questions

In the Bible, whenever a colour is mentioned, the writers are telling us something important about the person, place or thing which is colourful. Try using a Bible concordance (or Bible software); pick a colour and look up the different places that it appears. What significance is attached to that colour?

Let's pick one colour as an example: purple. It is mentioned in these two verses:

Luke 16:19 (NRSV): 'There was a rich man who was dressed in purple and fine linen and who feasted sumptuously every day.'

John 19:2 (NRSV): 'And the soldiers wove a crown of thorns and put it on his head, and they dressed him in a purple robe.'

What does purple tell us about where people think power lies?

Linear optics: lenses and the eye

Ratings

MESS ⚗   DANGER ⚗   DIFFICULTY ⚗

Theme

Anywhere in the Bible where it mentions eyes, seeing or vision

Equipment needed

A variety of lenses: magnifying glasses, microscopes, telescopes, binoculars, spare pairs of glasses (ideally, distance glasses – and the worse the eyesight, the better for this activity); some glasses cleaning wipes

Before you begin

Lenses bend light rays. We have two highly adaptable lenses in our eyes which bend light rays from both near and far objects so that the image is formed on our retinas. When our eyes start to fail, or need a boost, we turn to external lenses.

You may need to prepare a good couple of weeks in advance by asking around your church to borrow things containing lenses. Do explain that the plan is to be hands-on with the lenses, and check that people are happy with that. Alternatively, if their camera or telescope is really expensive, then invite them along to demonstrate it.

Experimental method

Let people examine and look through the lenses. What can they see? For example:

- Do they make things look bigger or smaller?
  Get people to vary the distance between the object and the lens – which way up is the image?
  Can distance glasses be used as a magnifying glass?
  What shape are the lenses?
  What different lenses are used in telescopes, microscopes, etc.?
- Can you spot the difference between distance and reading glasses?

Big thinking

There are two basic lens shapes. Those which are thinnest at the edge and thickest in the middle are called convex or converging lenses and can magnify. Those which are thickest at the edge and thinnest in the middle are called concave or diverging lenses and diminish the image. Short-sighted (or myopic) people use a concave lens (see photos online). Long-sighted (or hyperopic) people use a convex lens (see photos online).

Lenses bend light rays by slowing light down. You have probably heard that the speed of light is constant: strictly speaking, the speed of light *in a vacuum* is constant. The speed of light passing through anything else – glass, plastic, water – is slower.

The material that a lens is made from is given a measure according to how much it slows down the light. This is called the refractive index. The larger the refractive index, the slower that light travels through the material. If you wear glasses and have the more expensive, ultra-thin, high-refractive index lenses, then you have paid to see the world an imperceptibly smaller fraction of a second after everyone else.

Big questions

Psalm 139:14 (NRSV) says, 'I praise you, for I am fearfully and wonderfully made.' Even the briefest of studies of the intricacy of the eye should lead us to a profound appreciation of the truth of that verse and from there on to praise of God, the Lord of creation.

We certainly notice when our eyesight starts to fail. If in Genesis 27, Isaac could have gone to a branch of a popular chain of opticians, then the Old Testament would have been very different. The inability to correct failing eyesight becomes a biblical theme to express a diminished spiritual vision (Psalm 69:3, Psalm 88:9). Paul told the Corinthians to expect a clearer spiritual vision: 'For now we see in a mirror, dimly, but then we will see face to face' (1 Corinthians 13:12, NRSV). Even Job in his darkest time could hold on to the promise of seeing a saviour: 'I will see him for myself. Yes, I will see him with my own eyes. I am overwhelmed at the thought!' (Job 19:27, NLT).

What does it mean 'to see' without using your eyes?

Flame tests: atomic excitation

Ratings

MESS 💡💡💡 DANGER 💡💡💡 DIFFICULTY 💡💡

Theme

Immanence; indwelling; the presence of God

Equipment needed

A chemistry set with actual chemicals (can be sourced online)

Or: a flame source (meths burner, cook's blowtorch, etc. Do not use candles as they are too sooty); several large needles, preferably with large eyes; several corks; distilled water; salt (sodium chloride); bicarbonate of soda (sodium bicarbonate); cream of tartar (potassium bitartrate); nu-salt (potassium chloride)

Before you begin

Many chemicals look the same – this is part of their danger – and many are just plain white powders. How do we tell them apart if they are not labelled? Science has many analytical techniques for determining which elements are within a compound. This experiment uses flame testing to identify the type of metal atoms in the chemicals.

Do people like fireworks? Maybe the colours, if not the loud bangs. The different colours in fireworks are created by the same process that we will be experimenting with today. You could show a video of fireworks.

Whilst gloves would normally be used when working with chemicals, as we are using naked flames the hazard of setting fire to the gloves is probably the greater risk. We will build special flame test probes so there is not any need for the chemical to come into contact with the skin.

Experimental method

If you have bought a chemistry set, then follow the instructions in it instead of the ones below.

Stab the needles into the corks. (You will hold the cork and use the eye of the needle to place the chemical samples in the flames.) Clean the needles in fresh water to remove any contamination and then dry them. Test the needle for contamination by placing them at the edge of the flame and looking for any colour change.

Dip the eye of the needle in some distilled water and then into one of the chemicals. Hold the chemical sample in the edge of the flame. Note the colour change of the flame. Using the table below, identify the main metal in the chemical.

Boron	Bright green
Calcium	Orange-red
Copper	Green-blue
Iron	Gold
Potassium	Light purple to red
Magnesium	Bright white
Sodium	Bright yellow
Selenium	Bright blue
Strontium	Crimson red

Bicarbonate and cream of tartar are both white powders; challenge people to identify which is which by using the flame test. Again, table salt and nu-salt are both white crystalline powders; challenge people to identify which is which by using the flame test.

If you have a chemistry set, you will have the opportunity to look for additional flame colours other than just yellow and purple-red.

Big thinking

Even if the rest of the science in this section scares you off, at least marvel at this: in this experiment, we have reached inside an atom and caused sub-atomic particles to move!

One of the simplest models of an atom is called the Rutherford-Bohr Model, where the inside of an atom can be viewed like a mini solar system: the atom's nucleus (with protons and neutrons) is at the centre like a sun, with the electrons orbiting like planets.

The electrons cannot exist just anywhere, but only in specific shells around the nucleus. When we heat up the atom, the electrons take in energy, and jump up to the next shell. When the atom cools down, the electron jumps down and gives off a photon of light (these are the colours we saw). Each photon contains a quantum of energy.

Big questions

The English word 'atom' derives from the Ancient Greek word for 'uncut' or 'indivisible'. This is because in the world view of the Ancient Greeks, the atom was the smallest thing there could be: it couldn't be split. The Ancient Greek word occurs once in the Bible. In 1 Corinthians 15:52, the phrase 'in a moment' (NRSV) or 'in a flash' (NIV) is the Greek *en atomos*, an indivisible time.

Within an atom, the nucleus is actually (relatively) quite small. The electrons are even tinier. Depending on the atom, maybe 99.99999% of the atom is therefore empty space. You are made of atoms: you are 99.9999% nothing! 'What are human beings that you are mindful of them, mortals that you care for them?' (Psalm 8:4, NRSV).

With that much empty space inside, have you ever considered what that means for the Holy Spirit dwelling within you? When you think of God being present, do you only think of him in the space outside of you?

Fluorescence, iridescence and luminescence

Ratings

MESS DANGER DIFFICULTY

Theme

Knowledge, wisdom, proverbs

Equipment needed

This is a pick 'n' mix activity:

For an investigation of fluorescence: a dark room; an ultraviolet light (available from Maplin, etc.); any of: fluorescent pens, jelly made from tonic water, washing-up liquid, e.g. Persil non-bio, invisible inks/security markers

For an investigation of iridescence: a dark room; any of: bubble mixture, engine oil (a tiny amount), CDs and DVDs, some seashells

For an investigation of luminescence: a dark room; any of: glow-in-the-dark paint, glow-in-the-dark stars, glow sticks

Before you begin

It is possible that scientists used long words just to make themselves sound clever – I do love the way that 'iridescence' rolls off the tongue. But the technical words do help to describe accurately what we observe in the world.

Ask whether people know the meaning of the words in this chapter title. You could also ask whether there are any really long church words that they don't understand. Maybe start with a challenge to think of the longest word they know: 'Antidisestablishmentarianism' may not be suitable depending on your denomination (ask your vicar); but maximum points for 'floccinaucinihilipilification' (look it up in a really big dictionary).

Make sure the room you are in is sufficiently dark for these experiments to work.

Experimental method

Investigating fluorescence

Fluorescent things absorb light at shorter wavelengths, such as ultraviolet (UV), which the eye cannot see, and emit light at wavelengths that the eye can see. They appear to glow brighter but only whilst you shine the UV light on them. Use the UV light to find things which fluoresce.

1 Try different types of felt-tip pens.
2 The quinine in tonic water will fluoresce so you can make a jelly which glows eerily under UV light.
3 Many detergents contain optical brighteners which strongly fluoresce; you can use Persil to draw pictures that only appear under UV light.
4 Send messages using invisible ink (see photo online).

Investigating iridescence

Iridescent things emit a rainbow of colours which changes as they move around in the light. The white light is split by microscopic structures on the surface. Iridescence is generated by surfaces. See what iridescent things you can find.

1 Blow bubbles and, instead of popping them, observe their apparent colour as they float around.
2 You can replicate a car spilling oil on a wet road and see the same colours.
3 The microscopic pits used to store data on a DVD or CD create iridescence (see photo online), as do the structures on seashells and the wings of butterflies.
4 The shimmer of certain fabrics is iridescence.

Investigating luminescence

Luminescent (or phosphorescent, if you prefer Greek to Latin) things emit light over a longer timescale and after any external stimulus has been removed without generating any heat. Glow-in-the-dark things absorb light and then emit it much more slowly. Glow sticks use a chemical reaction to generate the light.

Have some fun exploring things that glow in the dark.

Big thinking

Much of science, physics in particular, is concerned with energy: producing it, controlling it and storing it. Actually, energy cannot be created or destroyed, only transformed from one form to another.

Big questions

Language is important in any field. The church has equally long words; try transubstantiation or consubstantiation (ask your vicar). There has long been a danger within the church of people thinking that they need special knowledge or special language to be a Christian. Our faith in Jesus is the most important thing we know; what is the best way to explain it?

Young's double slit experiment

Ratings

MESS   DANGER   DIFFICULTY

Theme

Wondering; revelation; who God is; incarnation

Equipment needed

Nit comb; laser pen; black electrical tape; a white piece of paper to form a screen

Before you begin

Thomas Young (1773–1829) made many contributions to the advancement of science; arguably the most significant was his wave theory of light, which overturned the particle theory of light that had stood since Isaac Newton's (1643–1727) *Opticks*. When he introduced this experiment to the Royal Society in 1803, he said, 'The experiment that I am about to relate... may be repeated with great ease.' See if you agree.

Do not buy cheap laser pens off the internet. A laser pen from a reputable source such as Maplin will be certified as class 2 and considered eye-safe, if you follow the instructions. Cheap, uncertified laser pens can blind you!

Remember the warning in the introduction – never look at bright light sources directly.

Experimental method

(See photos online.) Position the laser so that it shines on the paper screen at a distance of about a metre or so. (Taping it down so that it does not move helps with the set-up.) Note the pattern of the light. It should be a spot. Put the nit comb in the path of the laser beam so the light shines through the teeth of the comb. Note how the pattern has changed; it will now be a long row of short lines.

Ask people why they think the pattern has changed. They may say it is because the light is shining through all the gaps in the comb. Use the black tape to cover all but two of the gaps. Shine the laser through these two gaps and note the pattern. It should still be the long row of short lines. Ask people if they can think how just two gaps can produce this pattern.

Big thinking

Young's experiment conclusively demonstrated that light is a wave, like a wave on the ocean. The pattern of dark and light bands is called an interference pattern. When a wave hits a barrier with two small gaps, two smaller waves are produced on the other side of the barrier. These two new waves mix together. When the peaks of each wave mix together you get the bright spot; when the troughs of each wave mix, you get the dark spot.

Experiments by later scientists demonstrated conclusively that light is a particle which we call the photon; each photon or light particle contains one quantum of energy. The Open University has a nice video discussing this called 'Paradox of wave-particles', which you can search for online.

So is light a wave, like a wave on the ocean stretched out over space, or a particle, with the energy all in one spot? The best answer science has so far is: yes. Light is both, at the same time: unless you perform an experiment when you will find it is only one. This is the paradox of wave/particle duality.

Big questions

In Dr Dave's introduction, he writes, 'Science is often seen as a matter-of-fact exercise, explaining how things are.' Let us immediately dispel that notion when it comes to quantum theory. Here, we are right on the edge of human knowledge.

Notice how, when we approach the limits of human knowledge, the same struggles to find the right language appear. In the discussion of whether light is fully a wave or fully a particle, do you see any of the same shortfalls in language that we use to discuss Jesus? How can he be fully divine and fully human? If we don't use words for these 'mysteries', what language can we use? What language do churches use other than words?

Perspective

Anna Pearson studied Physics at Royal Holloway and is now a PhD student at Oxford working on quantum physics.

God and nature have always been part of my life. Some of my earliest memories are talking to God before falling asleep as a small child, and one of my absolute favourite things in nature are horses. I wouldn't say that I was a particularly 'sciencey' kid (or teenager); I did physics A level just to keep my options open and would not have taken someone seriously if they had suggested that I'd be doing a DPhil investigating quantum physics six years later.

I had no intention of studying science at university, but six months before leaving school I learnt about quantum mechanics through a DVD my physics teacher gave me to watch. I couldn't sleep that night. I really, really could not believe what I had just heard – things could seemingly be in two places at once, but only when you weren't watching (observing) them! This could not be true! There must have been a mistake. Didn't these silly scientists realise that common sense just would not allow this? I had to get to the bottom of it, so my university application changed and physics it was. Six years later and I'm still trying to better understand some of the mysteries in quantum mechanics; it doesn't look like I'll be twiddling my thumbs anytime soon, and perhaps not even getting a satisfactory answer in my lifetime.

I'm an experimental physicist (in training). This wasn't a job I ever considered or was even aware of as a child. I love what I do and rarely, if ever, have a chance to get bored! What I do varies a lot from day to day but it may include any of: reading some of the newest publications to keep up to date with what other scientists in my field have found out recently; planning, making, building or taking data on my current experiment; problem solving if things didn't go as planned; talking with other scientists to share ideas and think of new things to try out; analysing data and trying to understand what was going on; occasionally giving talks about what I do; and there is always more to learn and find out!

For me, the most inspiring verse in the whole Bible when it came to having the discipline to study for my exams during my first degree was Romans 1:20:

For since the creation of the world God's invisible qualities – his eternal power and divine nature – have been clearly seen, being understood from what has been made, so that people are without excuse.

My time spent with my textbooks was time spent delving into what has been made, time spent delving into God's eternal power and divine nature. What a privilege to live in an age where this is possible, where food for many can be produced by few, to free up time to be able to delve deep into the mysteries of creation. And trust me, there are many. In school you may get the impression that 'science' knows everything, but in reality there is so much we don't know, so much still to find out.

How have my studies impacted my faith?

In my GCSE years, I'm afraid to say that I actually spent a lot of time arguing back with my physics teachers. I thought that the earth was only 6,000 years old and that one had to take the start of Genesis as six literal 24-hour days. I thought I was a very dutiful Christian (indeed a 'proper' one, who took the Bible seriously!) arguing with teachers, disrupting the lesson and debating for endless hours on the school bus home. I now look back at this time and groan when I think of my immense arrogance and pride.

God took me on a humbling journey which started with me realising that my 16-year-old self might not have been quite right about everything. For the first thing, time is 'wibbly wobbly'; it can stretch and contract depending on various things such as how fast you are travelling and the gravitational field strength where you are. Also, time has a beginning and God didn't, so therefore he is outside of time, and for him a thousand years are like a day. So, digesting all of this, I had to come to the conclusion that perhaps there was more than one way of reading Genesis 1 while still being faithful to the message contained in the text.

The next biggie was evolution; I just could not swallow it. It wasn't until after three years of university that God challenged me on this one. I won't go into it here but for anyone who also finds it difficult I would recommend Denis Alexander's *Creation or Evolution: Do we have to choose?* (Monarch Books, 2008). It really challenged me, and stretched my view of God. He became bigger, not smaller as I had previously thought about a God who may have used evolution to fulfil his purposes. In fact, the question posed to Job in Job 40:8, 'Would you discredit my justice? Would you condemn me to justify yourself?' really pierced me to the core. If God is the author of creation, he has the right to do things in any way he should choose, and if his power has been on display since the creation of the world, then by studying it and understanding it we bring him glory, and *we do not need to fear what we might find*. From my current understanding of the Bible, two essential character traits of a Christian are humility and a thirst for the truth; these traits go hand in hand with a vocation/desire to spend one's working life doing science. As a church, let us encourage the younger ones to get stuck in!

5

Human body

Alex Bunn is a GP in London and also works for the Christian Medical Fellowship. But thankfully you won't need to read his handwriting in this book. He loves Messy Church because of the combination of down-to-earth playfulness, wonder and relationship it can foster.

Introduction

The human body is celebrated by both the arts and sciences: there is nothing more depicted in all of art, or as intriguing in all of science. And the good news is that all your participants should have the key piece of equipment: a body! Totally free, at the time of writing.

Recently, Western culture has tended to denigrate the body as being merely a machine, animal life or commodity. But, contrary to popular belief, the Bible gives us amazing reasons to celebrate our bodies: they are 'fearfully and wonderfully made' (Psalm 139:14), and can be 'temples' (1 Corinthians 6:19) where heaven and earth meet. God himself was happy to take on a human body like yours and mine, which gives everybody huge value and significance. The body of Christ was the first material object to be transformed, ready for the renewed world to come. Bodies have eternal significance like nothing else on the planet. No wonder the Bible uses the body as a rich metaphor for so many things!

Because many Bible stories are about human beings with all their physical needs, stories about the body appear all the way through. Some examples: Elijah being hungry, thirsty, running fast and being burnt out, imagery in the Psalms and in Job, Ezekiel's vision of the valley of dry bones, Jesus' birth, death and resurrection, his teaching about the body in Matthew 5—6, Lazarus being raised from the dead, any story about physical healing, the last supper, Paul's letters to the Romans (12) and Corinthians (1 Corinthians 12) and many other references in the epistles.

Heart: pump it up!

Ratings

MESS   DANGER   DIFFICULTY

Theme

Human technology is amazing, but God is even greater at making things. His greatest creation is people: we are fearfully and wonderfully made. The human heart is an impressive pump.

Equipment needed

Lamb or pig's heart (optional); sharp knife (if dissecting heart); small water bottle; 20 ml syringe; tape; scissors; glue; bowls

Before you begin

This experiment is about observing anatomy and physiology: how is the heart designed to work so efficiently?

- Start by asking: how big are our hearts? (Fist size.)
- Where are they? (Left side of the chest.)
- How long can they stop for? (Maximum two seconds before you pass out.)
- Try taking each other's pulses. How many times does your heart beat in a minute, year or lifetime? (100,000, 35 million and 2.5 billion; this is about double any other mammal.)
- How far does your blood travel each day? (20,000 km, which is the distance from London to Tokyo and back.)

Experimental method

If you are feeling adventurous, you could dissect an animal heart such as a pig or a lamb. A pig's heart is almost identical to a human's and costs just a few pence (be sensitive if you have people from Jewish or Muslim backgrounds; this may be less problematic if you are doing this experiment as a demonstration). It's certainly messy, and delightfully gory for some, as you point out the plumbing (arteries and veins), tendons ('heartstrings'), valves, and thick muscle on the left side which does the hardest work. If you can't identify these yourself, you can find plenty of easy-to-read diagrams by searching online.

Next, build a manual water pump. You can find videos online that show you how to do this, such as **www.youtube.com/watch?v=7ULcaaZGln8**. A simpler pump can be found at **www.youtube.com/watch?v=pPjS52Ee9Jc**. Simpler still, you could use pumps from soap dispensers.

See how much your group can pump in a minute. You could do this as a competition individually or in a team relay.

Big thinking

The heart is a double pump which moves blood around your body. It pumps blood to the lungs so that oxygen can be added to it. Then the blood returns to the other side of the heart, which pumps it out to the rest of your body, taking the oxygen with it. Your body needs oxygen to make energy to power it!

How much blood do you think our hearts pump in a minute, day and lifetime? (5 l, 7,000 l and 1 million barrels or 3 supertankers.) Which man-made machines can do this without stopping for over 100 years?

Big questions

What man-made things most impress you and why? What God-made things most impress you, and why? Can we make anything as impressive as the human body?

The prophet Ezekiel In chapter 36 talks about God taking away our hearts of stone and replacing them with hearts of flesh: what would be the problem with a heart of stone? When do you feel stony-hearted?

Brain: it's mind-blowing!

Ratings

MESS 💡💡💡💡💡   DANGER 💡💡💡💡💡   DIFFICULTY 💡💡💡💡💡

Theme

Human technology is amazing, but God is even greater at making things. His greatest creation is people: we are fearfully and wonderfully made. The human brain is astoundingly powerful.

Equipment needed

Poster to print out (see online); scissors; blu-tac; gold stars

Before you begin

The human brain does so much more than computer processing. But how does the brain compare with the computer for raw processing power? The answer may surprise you! Our brains are faster, smaller, cheaper and more powerful than the biggest computer in the world (so far). This is essentially an interactive quiz to demonstrate how amazing our brains are, even the smallest and slowest in the group, followed by a memory game to explore how well we can use the amazing power of the brain.

Experimental method

Display the poster (see online). Young people are pretty familiar with the digital world, but big numbers need illustrating. Ask participants where they would put familiar items like a DVD or mobile phone on a scale of data storage, and then ask them where they think the brain would fit.

Next, try to see how much of one of the biggest numbers we know – Pi (see 'A slice of Pi' on p. 239). This is a number that we think goes on forever – in 2016 it was calculated to 13 trillion decimal places – and never repeats. Here are the first 50:

3.14159265358979323846264338327950288419716939937510

You can calculate more decimal places on the website www.miniwebtool.com/first-n-digits-of-pi

See how many decimal places people can remember. Gradually increase the number of decimal places people try to remember, or work together in teams to see who has the best shared memory. Retest them after five minutes to see how much they can remember.

At the end of the activity, put gold stars on the foreheads of each of your participants, saying, 'Your brain is amazing!' Or as the Bible put it 3,000 years ago: 'You are wonderfully made' (Psalm 139:14).

If this activity is too short, you could combine with one of the others on the senses.

Big thinking

How clever is your brain? The answer is staggering: our brains can hold one petabyte (10 to the power of 15 bytes – a thousand million million or 10 with 15 zeros after it), slightly less than all the data that travels through Google worldwide every day (at the time of writing).

This is not the amount we can consciously remember, of course! It is the total storage capacity of the brain for all its functions. The brain has different types of memory. There is short-term memory, which repeats like a loop, over and over to help us remember things. Then there is long-term memory, which degrades unless it is accessed from time to time, so we forget things.

Big questions

Will a computer ever think and feel like a human? What's the difference?

Father of astronomy Johann Kepler wrote that science is 'thinking God's thoughts after him'. What do you think science is about?

Hearing: selective deafness (hearing impairment?)

Ratings

MESS  DANGER DIFFICULTY

Theme

We often miss things that are said. Sometimes we can't hear, sometimes we don't want to hear. Our hearing can sometimes even be selective.

Equipment needed

An online hearing test (you can find lots of free apps online); decent quality speakers or earphones; copy of chart on p. 120; tuning forks (optional); pipe-cleaners (optional)

Before you begin

Ask the group if they have noticed how some people's hearing is better than others. What factors are involved? Some may have noticed age, but see if they recognise ambient noise, pitch and distraction.

If you would like, you can play this short video before you test your group. Make sure the volume isn't too loud – you don't want to damage people's hearing! **www.channel.nationalgeographic.com/brain-games/videos/high-frequency-hearing-test**.

Experimental method

Test the highest frequency tone each person can hear, and plot frequency versus age (or age range if adults are shy about stating their age). It's good to admit that the young beat us in some areas! Record your scores and have a prize ready to give out to the winner.

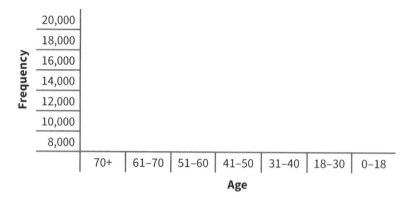

You could also supply some tuning forks and have a go at tapping each one on the table, to hear the different sounds produced. If you have access to a piano or a guitar, you could explore how different keys or strings make different noises.

Big thinking

Why can't we hear some things that others can? Mostly, it is due to degeneration in the inner ear from ageing.

Discuss hearing damage from loud music and earphones. Try not to sound too nagging, but this visual aid may help: hold a few pipe-cleaners in one hand and explain these are the hair cells in the inner ear that conduct sound to your brain. They work well when sound is at the right level (gently stroke the tops of the pipe-cleaners). But if noise is too loud, such as from earphones at full volume (bend the middle of the pipe-cleaners) they stop working (see photo online).

Big questions

James 1:22 asks whether we sometimes 'don't hear' when we are asked to do something we don't want to. For example, come to meals, go to bed, do jobs about the house, care for other people, or do our homework? Are there some subjects we don't like to talk about? Are there things that God may be telling us, that we don't want to hear? Does this get easier or harder as we get older?

It's easy to hear things around us, but how do you think we can hear from God?

Taste and see

Ratings

MESS 💡💡💡💡   DANGER 💡💡💡   DIFFICULTY 💡💡💡

Theme

Discernment (Matthew 15:11; 1 John 4:1; 1 Thessalonians 5:20–21)

Equipment needed

Plastic cups; LOTS of straws (you could cut these in half to make them more cost-effective); towels to catch drips; a range of sweet, sour (acid), bitter (like coffee), salt and umami (Bovril/Marmite) flavoured drinks; plastic sheet; fruit-flavoured Skittles

Before you begin

Make the Bovril/Marmite first as they need hot water to dissolve, and time to cool.

Ask for the group's favourite flavours. Ask if anyone knows about the taste map of the tongue (which actually shows which parts of the tongue taste different flavours more intensely – all parts of the tongue can taste all flavours). Ask if anyone has noticed how taste can be affected by having a cold, which blocks the sense of smell.

Experimental method

Set out plastic cups containing a number of edible but unlabelled liquids: cold coffee, cola, salt solution (3 g in 100 ml is about the same as sea water, so perhaps half this), Bovril/Marmite (check for vegetarians), lemon juice, orange juice, Ribena, sugar solution, etc.

Take a straw. Dip into the liquid, and place your finger over the other end firmly, raise, and then drop on to different parts of your tongue. What's the taste? Try not to laugh as people drip liquids everywhere; you may want to place a plastic sheet in the area.

For the second part of the experiment, get people to close their eyes, and pinch their nose. Then place a Skittle in their mouth, making sure they cannot see the colour. Ask them to say what the taste is – while holding their nose, many people will have difficulty doing this. Then, get them to let go of their nose. Can they tell the flavour now? Get them to describe what they experience. What does this say about our sense of taste?

Big thinking

The tongue is an amazing part of the body. It's made of a woven mat of muscles. In fact, it is one of the strongest in the body. Have you ever known your tongue to get tired? We use it to talk – and we use it to taste.

One hundred years ago, a German scientist called Hanig did an experiment to identify which parts of the tongue could taste four different flavours – sweet, salty, sour and bitter. He determined that the tip of the tongue tasted sweet and salty, the middle bit sweet and the back part bitter flavours. The sides tasted sour flavours (see **www.flavorfacts.org/wp-content/uploads/2013/10/umamitongue-1-500x270.jpg**).

From your experiments, do you think he was right? That's an important thing about science – whether what one person says they have found out in an experiment other people can find out by doing the same experiment. In fact, all parts of the tongue can taste all the different flavours, but maybe in different amounts or intensity. And, since Hanig did his work, a fifth flavour, umami, has also been identified.

In fact, taste and smell are very much linked together. When you let go of your nose while eating the sweet, you should have received an intense burst of flavour. Have you noticed that when we have a cold and a blocked nose, then our sense of taste is not very good?

Big questions

We have a sense of taste so that, when something comes into our mouth, we can decide to swallow it (if it tastes good), or spit it out (if it tastes bad). Ideas also come into us in a similar way; so how do we know which ideas are good or bad?

Read Psalm 34:8. What might it mean to 'taste and see that the Lord is good'?

Read James 1:16. Were you surprised by how easily your taste was deceived? How have you been tricked in everyday life? How can we avoid being tricked?

Get in touch

Ratings

MESS   DANGER DIFFICULTY

Theme

The power of touch

Equipment needed

For two-point discrimination: business cards; glue or tape; toothpicks

For the feel bag: a variety of small objects such as (easy) cup, spoon, ball, block, sponge, fruit, sponge, rock, cotton ball, leaf, pine cone, feather, or (difficult) wood letters, wood numbers, foil, peanuts, bar of soap

For sandpaper rankings: as many different grades of sandpaper as you can find

Before you begin

The two-point discrimination test has been used by real-life neurologists, and is the most scientific and measurable. Other modalities such as pressure, temperature and vibration are also medically useful. Feel bags and sandpaper are other fun ways to explore touch.

While doing the two-point discrimination experiment, be aware that toothpicks can be quite sharp. Tell your group not to put them anywhere near eyes or ears, or to run/be silly with them.

Ask your participants what kind of information skin can carry.

Experimental method

Two-point discrimination
Stick pairs of toothpicks on to the sides of two business cards with gaps of 60, 30, 15, 7.5 and 3.75 mm. Stick a final toothpick on to the remaining side by itself. Ask the participants whether they can discriminate (without looking) between the single toothpick and the paired toothpicks on various parts of the

body, such as back, arms, hands, legs, and feet, or even tongue. For each part, write down the smallest two-point gap they could differentiate as different to the single point.

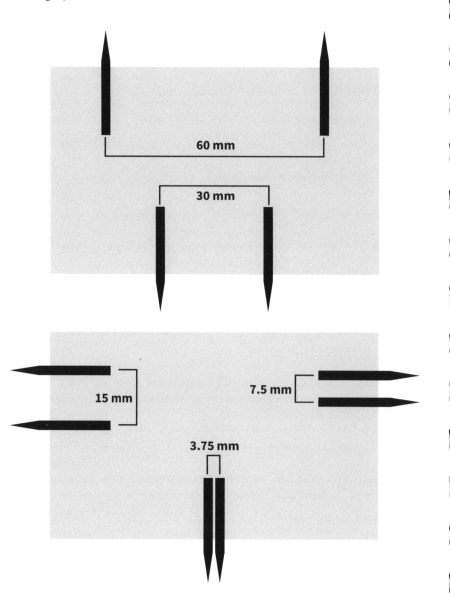

Feel bag

The aim is to identify a variety of objects by 'seeing their shape with fingers'. You can do this in several different ways, such as placing single items in a sock each, several into a pillowcase, or a fancier box with tunnels attached made from old socks to put hands through. To make it more challenging, race against the clock, show the item outside the box that needs retrieving by touch alone, or wear gloves of increasing thickness.

Sandpaper ranking

Cut small squares of different grades of sandpaper (which should have a measure of roughness somewhere on the back), and write a letter on the back of each corresponding to its rank. Jumble up the letters so you don't give the game away (i.e. don't write 1=A, 2=B, 3=C). You could stick the paper to wooden blocks. Then ask the members to rank the squares in order of roughness.

You can also test pressure with filaments of fishing line of different thickness, vibration with a tuning fork, and temperature with a hot water bottle.

Big thinking

Skin is the largest sense organ, which can surprise us with its sensitivity and power to connect us with each other. Did your skin surprise you? What kinds of information can skin convey? The answer is not simple, but includes pain, temperature, vibration, position, pressure, shape and a lot more in non-verbal communication.

Big questions

Read Luke 5:13. How does touch change the way we feel? Can you think of examples when you needed a touch from someone? Why did Jesus often touch people who others would not?

Read 1 John 1:1. What difference does it make that God decided to become man? Why do you think God wanted to be touchable?

Body unity

Ratings

MESS   DANGER   DIFFICULTY

Theme

The need for body parts to work together; the need for people to work together

Equipment needed

Part one: at least six volunteers; balloons; sweets; sticky tape; paper; markers

Part two: A4 pictures; scissors

Before you begin

Ask the group if anyone knows examples of how the body works by way of cooperation between its parts or organs.

Experimental method

Part one

This activity establishes how the body is made up of interconnected systems through acting out a dramatisation. You can be creative with costumes and props for each of the roles, which can be as simple as taping the role to the volunteer, with balloons for oxygen and carbon dioxide. You could also use background music such as 'Staying Alive' by the Bee Gees. Have all the actors stand in a ring, with each role stepping into the middle and serving the others in turn. Don't worry if it gets a little chaotic, the point is that every part is helping every other part all the time.

The **brain** (nervous system) instructs **arms** and **legs** (musculoskeletal system) to go to the kitchen to get a packet of sweets to eat (**digestive system**). The sugar is transported in the **blood** (circulatory system) to all other parts (take individual sweets round all the other systems). But how is **blood** being moved? That's why we need a **heart** (cardiovascular system) to push him round! But the **heart** looks a bit breathless; he needs the **blood** to fetch some oxygen from the **lungs** (respiratory system) still pushed by the **heart**. And all of this produces waste (every actor passes **blood** their sweet wrappers), which gets taken back to the **digestive system**.

Part two
This is a game of cooperation and can be done in teams against the clock. Make a simple jigsaw out of an A4 picture with only six to eight pieces. One volunteer is blindfolded and has to complete the jigsaw on the instructions of the rest of the team.

Big thinking
Which is the most important system in the body? How can any part work without all the others?

Big questions
How has God made us depend on each other?

1 Corinthians 12:17–21 says that every part of the body needs every other part of the body. How is this also true of parts of a family, church or country?

Blind spots

Ratings

MESS DANGER  DIFFICULTY

Theme

Seeing is believing, but our eyes often deceive us. We have 'blind spots' literally and spiritually, and some of the most important things in life are not seen by the eyes.

Equipment needed

Strips of paper; pens

Before you begin

There are lots of great optical illusions you can find online. You can choose a variety to suit a range of age groups, with explanations of the science that are age appropriate.

Experimental method

Give each person in the group a strip of paper. Get them to draw a dot on the left of the paper and a cross on the right of the paper (they should be about 15–20 cm apart). Now get them to close their left eye and look at the dot from about 50 cm (an arm's width) away. Gradually bring the paper closer to your eyes until the cross has disappeared. Try it again, this time closing your right eye and looking at the cross. As you bring the paper closer to your eyes, the dot will disappear.

Big thinking

Is seeing believing? Or are we easily deceived? The blind spot is actually the part of the retina which cannot detect light because this is where the optic nerve exits the eye to go towards the brain.

Big questions

Can we disbelieve what our eyes tell us? When is it right to? Why do people say that 'seeing is believing'? When should we not believe what we see in everyday life? Think about practical examples, such as hallucinations, magic shows or the false claims of advertising.

Conversely, the blind spot experiment showed us that we couldn't see things that were just in front of us. Did that surprise you? Are there everyday examples of people refusing to see what is 'right before their eyes'? For instance, a minority of people deny climate change. Why do people (including us) deny things we know to be true?

What other things do we believe in that we can't see? What did Jesus say about looking for evidence for faith? Contrary to popular opinion, Christian faith is based on believing evidence.

Ephesians 1:18 says the 'eyes of your heart' are as important as our physical eyes in deciding what is real and what is false. Why do some people believe things and others not?

In John 20:27–29, Jesus encouraged Thomas to see (examine evidence) and believe because of it. The Bible was written to help us who were not around to see Jesus with our own eyes. Read Luke 1:1–4. The Bible was written down as a reliable record, to see the world as it is. Luke was a doctor who wrote a Gospel based on thorough observation and research.

DNA extraction

Ratings

MESS   DANGER **DEMO ONLY**   DIFFICULTY

Theme

What makes you, you?

Equipment needed

A small clear plastic beaker; chilled water and chilled methylated spirits (available from hardware stores) – enough of each to fill a third of the beaker (place them in sealed bottles in a fridge overnight and try to keep cool before doing the experiment); disposable vinyl gloves; one teaspoon of salt; washing-up liquid; a teaspoon; wooden skewer; two strawberry laces, dolly mixtures and cocktail sticks (optional)

Before you begin

Ask people to suggest things that every animal and plant on the planet have in common.

Explain that every living creature on the earth has a very special chemical in every cell of the body. It is called DNA – Deoxyribonucleic Acid – you could have fun trying to get people to say it together. You get some of it from each of your parents and it determines a lot about what makes you, you: what colour your eyes and hair are; whether you look similar to your mum or dad, or even your Auntie Nellie; even whether you are a boy or girl!

In this experiment we are going to extract some DNA from some people.

Experimental method

Note: It is recommended that disposable vinyl gloves are worn for this experiment due to the handling of material from someone's mouth and also methylated spirits, which is toxic and a skin irritant. You may want to consider running it as a demonstration only.

Pour the chilled water into the beaker. Add the salt and stir with a spoon. Ask an adult to rinse their mouth out with the salt solution, swirling it around without swallowing it, and then spitting it back into the glass. To add to the mess, get them to do this twice!

Add a few drops of washing-up liquid into the water, stirring it around while trying not to make too many bubbles. Now, slowly pour the chilled methylated spirits into the beaker. As it is lighter than water, it will float on the liquid. Wait and watch, paying attention to where the water and methylated spirits meet. After a few minutes – perhaps as long as five or ten minutes if the liquids are not chilled enough – you should see a white substance form between the two liquids. Using the wooden skewer, try to wrap the substance around the skewer and draw it up out of the beaker. If you are careful, you can get a very thin thread forming. This is a thread of DNA.

Big thinking

While you are waiting for the DNA to appear, you could explain to your participants what is happening. It might help if you have a model of DNA, which can be made with two strawberry laces, cocktail sticks and dolly mixtures. Lay the laces next to one another and connect with the cocktail sticks, with two dolly mixtures on each stick. Now twist the laces to make a spiral.

Explain that DNA is what makes life possible. It is a beautiful chemical and it is in every cell of your body. The cells can unzip the spiral and then, using the food that you eat, can remake two copies. This is happening in our bodies all the time and it is how the body grows and renews itself when cells get worn out.

When the volunteer washed their mouth out, some of their cheek cells came off into the water. The DNA is in the centre of the cell – the nucleus – and the salt in the water begins to release it. The cell is surrounded by a fatty skin, and in the same way as when we do the washing-up, the washing-up liquid helps to break down the fatty barrier and release the DNA into the water.

DNA can dissolve in water, but not in alcohol, so where the water and methylated spirits meet, the DNA becomes a solid. The thin thread of DNA that is pulled out is made up of millions of different strands of DNA. A typical cell in your body has 2 m of DNA, tightly squashed up into 46 bunches called chromosomes.

Big questions

Jesus said that 'the very hairs of your head are all numbered' (Matthew 10:30). Science tell us that that there is a staggering amount of information packed into each tiny hair and every cell in the body. What does amazing DNA tell us about God's attention to detail, and how he cares for us? How does that make you feel?

Messy fingerprints

Ratings

MESS 💡💡💡💡💡   DANGER 💡💡💡💡💡   DIFFICULTY 💡💡💡💡💡

Theme

God has made each person unique. Science can identify individuals in many ways including fingerprints. God has left evidence ('fingerprints') of his unique character on his creation.

Equipment needed

A bottle or flat sheet of plastic on which to make prints; dusting powder (or alternative such as baby powder); make-up brush; clear sticky tape (the wider the better); a sheet of clear plastic; a magnifying glass; dark paper

Before you begin

This is worth practising ahead of time, as there is some technique involved. Ask someone in advance to place a fingerprint on to a clean plastic or glass surface. It's grease that sticks to the powder, so it helps to make the finger slightly greasy first, by rubbing on the nose or forehead.

Ask if anyone knows how fingerprints are taken.

Experimental method

You could start by getting each participant to make their own fingerprints using ink on paper (see photo online). Be careful not to have too much ink on your finger, as it will work less well. Ink-free baby print packs are also available. See if people can spot the subtle differences between them: one finger may not be enough.

Next, demonstrate to the group how to take prints. Dust the plastic or glass surface (on which someone has already placed their fingerprint) with a little powder and remove the excess with the make-up brush in swirling, dabbing or sideways strokes. Transfer this print by applying wide clear tape to it and sticking it on to the clear plastic. To help visualise the print, lay the clear plastic over dark paper. A magnifying glass will be useful, or if you own an OHP these transmit quite well, or you could photograph and display on a larger screen.

After demonstrating, let your group try to capture the same person's prints left on other surfaces. You can then compare this fingerprint with a bank of fingerprints taken from other leaders: see who can identify which leader left the fingerprints. Younger eyes are impressively good at identifying suspects!

Big thinking

This is a very old technique which is still used to solve crimes today. What techniques helped to get the best print and match?

Big questions

God has his 'fingerprints' all over his creation, evidence of design, beauty and order. Science can help to reveal and celebrate these. Where have you seen his fingerprints? What might this tell us about the God who created the universe?

For the older members, here is a major question about science and faith: what problems are there in looking for God only in his works (the material world) as opposed to his word (how he has shown himself in history and the Bible)? Evolution and the observation of suffering in nature are likely to come up.

See Psalm 19:1 and Romans 1:20 for where God reveals himself in creation (or nature). See Colossians 1:15–16 for how God most clearly reveals himself in history, especially in Jesus.

Dem bones

Ratings

MESS DANGER DIFFICULTY

Theme

The functions of bones; bone health

Equipment needed

Lollipop sticks; sticky tape; chicken bones; vinegar

Before you begin

Soak some chicken bones in vinegar at least four days in advance.

Experimental method

Start with some skeleton questions: which are the biggest and smallest bones? (Femur in thigh and stapedius in inner ear.) Which is most commonly broken? (Radius in wrist.) How many bones do you have? (300 at birth, 206 by maturity at 25.) Which has more bones in its neck, a man or a giraffe? (The same, seven.)

So why do we have bones? Well, if we didn't, we would be jellyfish, and not be able to stand up and move.

To show how important bones and joints are, tape lollipop sticks to a volunteer's finger, and challenge them to perform some simple task, such as writing, sharpening a pencil or tying shoelaces. This will be much harder because you cannot use your joints to bend your fingers.

Then, to explore bone health, take the chicken bones that have been soaked in vinegar, which dissolves the mineral content (mostly chalk, calcium carbonate). Without this, the bones are much softer and weaker than bones that have not been soaked in vinegar (have some available for comparison). You can also demonstrate the other parts of the bone such as marrow, which produces blood cells, safely protected within.

Optional: As a child I was fascinated by a book of animal skeletons. Use an online quiz or a library book to see if your participants can guess the animal from the skeleton.

Big thinking

Why should we be thankful for our bones? Has anyone broken a bone? How did that affect you? How did it feel to have your joints immobilised? How do we look after our bones? (Dairy products provide the calcium to keep them strong, and exercise also reminds the body to keep reinforcing them.)

Big questions

Every tiny part of your body has been lovingly designed and created by God. How amazing is that?

Read Luke 14:13. What was Jesus' attitude to people with disabilities?

Perspective

Amy Johnson studied natural sciences at Cambridge, and is now a PhD student at Cambridge working on the neuroscience of child development in deprived areas.

Having a science teacher for a father, my childhood was filled with making rockets, setting fire to strange metals and the encouragement to be curious about the world and why it is the way it is. I grew up with a love of science and an understanding that it can tell us more about who God is and how amazing he is. As I studied science at school and physics at the University of Cambridge, I found that the more I learnt about science, the more I felt awe and wonder at God and his creation and my faith and relationship with him grew.

At the same time, I was learning that God has put us here on earth with the purpose of making a positive difference in the lives of the people around us. The Bible is full of passages in which God commands us to demonstrate his love through actions such as healing the sick, taking care of his creation and giving to the poor. I find a passage in Isaiah 58 particularly inspiring in which God tells us that the kind of worship he really wants from us is to 'break the chains of injustice, get rid of exploitation in the workplace, free the oppressed, cancel debts… [share] your food with the hungry, [invite] the homeless poor into your homes' (vv. 6–7, *THE MESSAGE*). I had a growing conviction that this was the work I was called to do and so, as I was coming to the end of my degree and trying to decide what to do next, I was faced with a dilemma: to pursue science or social action?

I was in the middle of praying about this decision when the Savar garment factory in Bangladesh collapsed, killing over 1,000 workers; one of the deadliest structural accidents in the history of humankind. The thought that so much could have been done to prevent the exploitation, oppression and ultimately the death of so many left me feeling that I couldn't do anything other than work in the area of social action. I made what I thought was the decision to leave science behind for good and signed up to work as a community intern at my church.

One of my main tasks was to set up a new project targeting child poverty, a big issue in the area surrounding our church. As I researched the ways we could make a difference in this, I was surprised to discover that people all over the world were using science to investigate child poverty and influence governments, charities, churches and schools to help them make the most effective difference possible. I had a revelation: I didn't have to choose! I could use what I really loved doing, scientific research, to make a big difference in what I was really passionate about, child poverty.

I'm now in the final year of my PhD, investigating how child poverty affects our brain development. We know that the environment that we grow up in has a profound impact on almost every area of our development, setting the trajectory of our lives. However, we also know that some children show a remarkable resilience to the negative effects of growing up in a deprived environment. We want to understand why some children are more at risk, and what gives children resilience from these risks so that we can make a positive impact in the lives of children growing up in poverty.

I believe that science is an incredible tool that we can use to live out God's command to make a difference in this world. Whatever the issue, whether it's using neuroscience to tackle poverty, medical research to treat illnesses, food science to solve hunger, conservation to counteract climate change or social research to fight against injustice, science can enable us to find the best solutions to every need, giving us the potential to make a big difference in the lives of many people.

6

Plants

Graham Hartland is a clergy spouse, father of a multi-talented musician and in his spare time heads up the Biology department in a secondary school. He has taught since 1992, run children's work since 1988 and in the summer can be found, armed with a macro lens, chasing insects on the heaths of Hampshire.

Introduction

Plants are interesting; they are the unsung heroes of creation. All life rests on their endeavours: they provide food, shelter, materials for building, clothes, drinks, dyes, fertiliser, medicines, fuel, transport, recreation, measure time and, of course, provide the vital oxygen we need to stay alive. In these activities, we explore some of these aspects, as well as see how plants help us to understand the amazingness of God, ourselves and each other.

Bible stories involving plants include creation, the tree of life, the ten plagues, Jonah's vine, references to vineyards, Jesus' many parables about seeds and the lilies of the field.

Tree rings

Ratings

MESS 💡💡 DANGER 💡💡 DIFFICULTY 💡

Theme

Trees are good for time travel – they are a record of what conditions were like in years gone by

Equipment needed

Tree trunk; magnifying glasses; small nails 5–8 cm long; sticky labels; hammer (any size will do); pens/felt-tip pens; sticky tape

Before you begin

Why do trees have rings? The paler wide rings show fast growth, and are made of bigger cells. The darker narrow rings show slow growth and are made of smaller narrower cells. These rings can be seen using a magnifying glass. Each pair of dark and light rings is a year's worth of growth. To make this activity worthwhile, you'll need a trunk with at least 40 rings.

Experimental method

This is an expedition into memory. The last ring was when the tree was cut down, so label this outer ring (not the bark) with the year the tree was cut down. Get people to write their year of birth and name on a label. Stick the label to a nail and hammer it into the correct ring. (See photos online.)

What events can they remember: year of marriage? Year they moved house? Year they started school? Year they took part in the pantomime? Write the event on a label and nail it into the correct ring. You now have a timeline of your participants' lives!

Big thinking

Why are the rings different sizes? Use the magnifying glass to check that the cells are different sizes. What might make the trees grow quicker in the summer and slower in the autumn and spring? Will there be any growth during winter? Cold temperatures will make the plants grow slowly, whilst warmer ones will speed up growth.

Big questions

When do we grow best? What sorts of things help us? What about our spiritual growth? Or how do we grow more kind? Can people see us growing in love? Trees have rings to show how they have grown, so what evidence is there for our growth?

Fruit batteries

Ratings

MESS 💡💡💡💡 DANGER 💡💡💡💡 DIFFICULTY 💡💡💡💡

Theme

Humble things working together can be a source of amazing energy

Equipment needed

Lemons or oranges; zinc pieces (e.g. galvanised nails); copper metal pieces (e.g. copper clout nails or piping); wires; crocodile clips; five-volt LEDs (Maplins code WL28F)

Before you begin

The two metals (zinc and copper) will generate a current if placed in acid. The current will flow from the more reactive metal (zinc) to the less reactive copper. This current is made up of electrons. If you have sufficient numbers of electrons moving, then you can light an LED.

Experimental method

(See photos online.) Cut the lemons or oranges in half. Gently squeeze the fruit to break some of the cells. Pierce one side of the fruit with a copper nail and pierce the other side with a zinc nail. Make sure that the two nails do not touch inside the lemon. Repeat several times until you have at least ten halves of lemon.

Use the wires to attach the copper of one lemon to the zinc of another lemon. This ensures that the lemons all push the electrons in the same direction! Repeat until all lemons are wired up, except for the first zinc nail and the last copper nail.

Attach a wire to the LED. The leg of the 'flat' side of the LED needs to be joined to the first zinc nail, and the other leg of the LED needs to be joined to the last copper nail. The LED should light, albeit dimly. If it's too dim, add more lemons to the circuit between the LED and the last copper nail.

Big thinking

The metals and acid work as a team to bring about a surprising outcome. And with more team members, the result looks brighter and brighter, as long as they push in the same direction.

Big questions

Working with others brings more energy than working by ourselves. Why is being involved with a church, a political party, a team, a class, a band, a family or an orchestra so important? What happens if people start to push against the team's direction?

Growing babies best

Ratings

MESS  DANGER DIFFICULTY

Theme

Taking care of each other; nurturing

Equipment needed

Cress or white mustard seeds; cotton wool or kitchen towel; plates (get a cheap set from a local charity shop); water; labels; individual egg holders, cut up from egg boxes; small freezer bags; metal 'twisty' closures

Before you begin

Plants need a variety of conditions to grow properly. This experiment examines how plants grow in different places.

At least a week in advance, place some cotton wool on a plate, make it really damp and add 20 seeds. Do this for several plates and place these in the airing cupboard, in a fridge, on several window sills, outside, under a saucepan, etc. You will need to water these every day, just to keep the cotton wool damp. You might also like to set up a second set which only gets water at the start and at the end. The plants in each condition will grow differently.

Create some labels with each different location, but don't stick them on to the plates.

Experimental method

Bring the plants and the labels to the event. Get people to try to link the plant with the label, and talk about why they made the decision.

Give each participant a cut-up egg box, some cotton wool, around ten seeds and the plastic bag. Ask them how they might make the perfect home for plants. Place the cotton wool and seeds into the egg box, dampen a little, and place into the plastic bag. Seal the bag with a metal twisty closure to stop the bits from falling out.

Big thinking

Plants by a window will grow towards the light. This is called phototropism. Plants in the dark will be etiolated: yellow, grow tall and spindly. Plants with less water will not grow as well, especially in hot weather! Cold temperatures will make the plants grow slowly, whilst warmer ones will speed up growth.

Big questions

How could you grow the perfect plant? Where are you going to place yours? So what are the perfect conditions to grow people? How could you grow better? What stops us growing?

Starch testing

Ratings

MESS ☺☺☺☺☺   DANGER ☺☺☺☺☺   DIFFICULTY ☺☺☺☺☺

Theme

Making the hidden visible

Equipment needed

A variety of foods like potatoes, rice, pasta, biscuits, bread, apple, onions; iodine solution; pipettes; plastic sheets; newspaper to cover plastic; aprons; disposable paper plates; bowls

Before you begin

Iodine can stain, so keep it away from clothes!

Experimental method

Cover the table and floor with plastic sheets and place newspaper on top of the plastic sheet (to stop the iodine soaking through in case of spills). Suggest (strongly) that participants wear aprons to protect their clothes.

Place chopped-up pieces of the foods in individual bowls. Allow participants to take a few of the foods and place them on the plates. Use the pipettes to drip iodine on to the foods. After a few seconds, the foods which contain starch will turn black. (See photos online.)

Big thinking

Iodine can detect whether there is any starch in a food. This is because starch is made of long curly molecules. The iodine gets stuck in the curls and causes a colour change from brown to a bluey-black colour.

Starch is a good source of energy, being a carbohydrate. Athletes will 'carbo load' before a race so that their body contains sufficient carbohydrates. These are then used in respiration to release the energy needed to power the muscles.

Big questions

What sorts of things are hidden? What things should not be hidden? The role of the Holy Spirit is to uncover what is hidden. Colossians 1:26 (ESV) talks about 'the mystery hidden for ages and generations but now revealed to his saints', and 1 Corinthians 2:7–8 says, 'We declare God's wisdom, a mystery that has been hidden and that God destined for our glory before time began. None of the rulers of this age understood it.' Do we understand what Jesus did? How could we make it clear?

Leaf rubbing

Ratings

MESS 💡💡   DANGER 💡   DIFFICULTY 💡

Theme

Finding the paths of life

Equipment needed

Leaves (best done in autumn); plain paper; coloured crayons; hard surface to press on

Experimental method

Get leaves – lots of leaves. Place each leaf on a hard surface and cover it with paper. Rub the paper with crayons, using as many colours as possible. (See photos online.) Make sure people's names go on these.

Award prizes for the loveliest/neatest, etc., using age categories if needed. Extra credit if people can name the leaves!

Big thinking

Different plants have different leaves. These are adapted to absorb as much light as possible so the plant can feed. The lines on the leaves carry water from the roots to the leaves, and also carry sugars from the leaves (where they are made) to other parts of the plant. Plants rely on their different parts to function properly, just like people.

Big questions

Paul talks about the church being the body of Christ (Romans 12:4–5, 1 Corinthians 12:27): all members of one body. So if the church is a plant, are you a leaf (provider of food), a root (support, sucking up life-giving water), the stem (everything hangs on me, I'm a conduit and pass things on) or a flower (I'm here to attract people to church/just here to look pretty/I fade fast when it gets too hot…)? With younger children, you might consider, 'Which kind of leaf is your favourite?', 'Do you think you'd like to be a leaf or would you rather be a root, a flower or a stem? Why?'

Camouflage

Ratings

MESS   DANGER DIFFICULTY

Theme

Hiding in plain sight; being distinctive

Equipment needed

Hole punch; range of papers, like graph paper or plain white or coloured paper, to hole punch; range of papers in ONE colour for the actual activity; containers e.g. screw top jars; tweezers/forceps/clothes pegs (optional); stopwatch

Before you begin

Have fun hole-punching sheets of paper. You will generate lots of dots of paper. You will want to put these into containers, one for each time you want the activity to run. To make this a scientific experiment, make sure that there are the same number of paper dots of each colour in each container.

Experimental method

Open a container and sprinkle the dots over several sheets of the same colour paper. Give a countdown, then allow the participants 30 seconds to gather as many paper dots as they can. If you have older participants, consider only allowing them to pick up the dots with an implement. Count the dots. Which colour was collected most? If you used the tweezers/forceps/clothes pegs, then which implement gathered the most dots?

Sweep the used dots into a bin, have the discussion, and then set up the next round of activity using fresh paper dots. (You will need fresh dots each time because old ones get folded and therefore are easier to pick up second time round.)

Big thinking

Plants grow happily, and provide camouflage for animals to hide in from either prey (grasshoppers, tree frogs, etc.) or predators (lions, cheetahs, etc.) You will find that the dots which stand out are more likely to be spotted and picked up. The ones which are the same colour as the background are less likely to be picked up.

Big questions

Should Christians hide in society (1 Timothy 2:2, ESV: 'a peaceful and quiet life'; 1 Thessalonians 4:11, NLT: 'goal to live a quiet life') or be distinctive (Matthew 5:15: 'Neither do people light a lamp and put it under a bowl. Instead they put it on its stand, and it gives light to everyone in the house')? How can Christians change society for the better? What would the perfect Christian do? How might the church help the local community to make it more distinctive? How could you help the community?

All you need in a seed

Ratings

MESS  DANGER DIFFICULTY

Theme

Can we predict what a plant will look like from its seeds?

Equipment needed

Seeds (you could use: cress, white mustard, bean, tomato, carrot, fennel, coriander, acorn, coconut); pictures of the plants they produce, in colour and laminated; small bowls; sticky tape/blu-tack

Before you begin

Seeds are amazing, as they contain the baby plant and sufficient stored food to grow roots and a shoot for as long as it takes to grow out of the ground and reach the light.

Experimental method

Stick the adult plant pictures on to one set of bowls and have piles of seeds in another set of bowls. Get participants to have a think and decide which seed matches which adult plant. Vote by placing the seed in the relevant bowl. (Make sure younger children do not try to eat the seeds.)

Big thinking

Just because seeds are small does not always mean the adult plant is small. The food store really tells you how deep the seed can be planted – small seeds must be planted either on the surface of the soil or not too deeply; big seeds travel a long distance or can be planted deeper in the soil.

Big questions

What kind of person might you grow into? Can you predict from what you've done so far what you might turn into? Are we limited by our upbringing? Our genes? What affects how we grow? The kingdom of God is like a mustard seed (see Matthew 13:31).

Yeast

Ratings

MESS 💡💡💡 DANGER 💡 DIFFICULTY 💡💡

Theme

A little yeast goes a long way

Equipment needed

Ingredients for dough (flour, water, yeast, sugar, salt); small mugs; source of hot water if it's a cold day

Before you begin

Make the dough before the meeting. Add different amounts of yeast to each dough, and add none to others. Divide the dough into blobs to be used later. You can do this by hand or by using a bread maker.

Experimental method

If it's cold, warm the mugs with hot water and then tip out the hot water. Place the dough blobs into the mugs. You will want to have them around half filled with the dough.

In which mugs does the dough expand the fastest? In which mugs does the dough not grow at all?

Optional: Take the risen dough out of the mugs, pop into a hot oven for 15–20 minutes and enjoy with butter. You might choose to decorate the dough with eyes, hedgehog spikes, etc.

Big thinking

Yeast is really millions of microscopic cells of a fungus which respire the sugar into mainly water and carbon dioxide; some alcohol is made as well. The carbon dioxide makes the dough rise. So the more yeast, the faster the dough rises, and fills the cup quicker. You don't get drunk eating bread as the alcohol quickly evaporates out of the dough in the oven.

Big questions

Yeast is alive. Bringing some life to the dough made it rise. Without that life, the dough just sits there and does nothing. So: in what ways do you bring life to a situation? Are there situations you can think of which need life adding to them to make them rise? Matthew 13:33 says, 'The kingdom of heaven is like yeast that a woman took and mixed into about sixty pounds of flour until it worked all through the dough.' Why might Jesus have referred to the kingdom of heaven as yeast?

Potato osmosis

Ratings

MESS   DANGER DIFFICULTY

Theme

Fragility; resilience

Equipment needed

Potatoes; mugs; salty water (three good teaspoons of normal salt in a mug of water is fine – if you use expensive sea salt, the crystals are quite big and may take a while to dissolve); fresh water; towels

Before you begin

Before the meeting, chop up the potatoes into chips around 7 cm long. You might want to ask for helpers! (Some helpers might want to use their own chips for their experiment, so be sure to label them if required.)

Around 20 to 30 minutes before your first group, put five potato chips in a mug of fresh water, and five chips in a mug of salty water. If you are doing this activity with more than one group, make sure you put the potatoes in the water with plenty of time before each group.

Experimental method

Examine fresh potato chips for bendiness and flexibility, and then take a look at the chips that have been in the two types of water for the last 20 to 30 minutes. Which ones are more flexible? Which ones weigh more? (See photos online.) Use the towels to dry your hands afterwards.

Big thinking

Osmosis is the movement of water through cell membrane from a dilute solution to a more concentrated solution. The chips in pure water will therefore absorb water and become stiffer as the cells 'inflate' (become turgid) with the incoming water. If bent too much, they will snap! Those in the salt solution will lose water, and thus will become more flexible. This is because the cells 'deflate' (become flaccid) as the water leaves them to go to the more concentrated salt solution.

Big questions

The salt causes water to move out of the potato, and makes it more flexible (look up osmosis again). So, what's moving into us to make us inflexible, causing us to snap (like this potato chip from the tap water mug); what can we do to be more flexible? Jesus suggests we should be salt in the world: how can we deal with those issues in society which appear to be inflexible or causing people to snap under pressure?

Survey the churchyard

Ratings

MESS DANGER  DIFFICULTY

Theme

Community; environment; stewardship

Equipment needed

Wellies; guidebooks to your local area (optional); colour pictures for treasure hunt (optional)

Before you begin

The danger rating will change depending on integrity of fences; access to roads; cars; location of sharp hazards (needles, nails, splintered wood); poisonous mushrooms; wild animals; wasps and bees (anaphylactic shock). You might want to walk around first to have a check. Remember you will need a suitable number of adults if you have children with your group.

After you have gone around yourself: what did YOU find? Identify it, so that you can QUICKLY answer the excited questions of your group. You might also like to make it into a treasure hunt.

Experimental method

Have fun by walking around your local area with your group, and see what you can find. Keep a record of 'what', 'where' and 'how much'.

Who can find the biggest variety of organisms? Who has found the most interesting organism? What makes it interesting?

Extra challenge: If you make it into a treasure hunt, then you will need to include colour pictures of the things to find. Get people to take photos of themselves with the organism so that there is proof they saw it.

Another challenge: Have a timed treasure hunt for older people.

Big thinking

Living things make this planet. Each of them has a role, a place on the earth to do a particular job. Each one has a particular set of adaptations to help it fulfil its role – thorns to help climb up, large leaves to collect light, roots to collect water.

Big questions

Why are there so many organisms? What can we do to preserve them? You could even use the idea of being 'fearfully and wonderfully made' (Psalm 139:14) – this does not just apply to humans: all of creation is deemed at least 'good' (Genesis 1:31)! What happens if a species becomes extinct? How can we improve our environment to keep species alive? How do we show respect to God through how we treat his planet?

Perspective

Revd Jennifer Brown is the Science Missioner in the Churn Benefice, a group of churches in the Diocese of Oxford.

My work is all about building relationships between science and Christianity. This is definitely a two-way system; talking to people who work in science and technology to help them see that religion isn't anti-science, and talking to people in the church to help them see the ways in which science gives us another window through which we can catch glimpses of God. In my work as Science Missioner, I often find myself using scientific ideas to help others discover new ways to think about God. I also try to bring Christian thinking to bear on current issues in science, especially in relation to ethical questions.

I grew up in a churchgoing family, so God has always been a part of my life. I've been fascinated by science since childhood, too. I don't think there has ever been a time when I felt that the two didn't or couldn't go together. I was lucky in that I grew up just outside Washington, D.C. in the USA, and so my childhood had many trips to the Smithsonian Institution. Its Museum of Natural History was one of my favourite places (the Air and Space Museum was another).

At about the age of four, I decided I wanted to be a doctor when I grew up, and I've always loved biology. My interest in medicine stayed with me, and I started university studying for a degree in biology. I ended up changing to psychology, and that's still my field today. Why did I change? Well, to be honest, it was chemistry that did it! I did well in the lab, but really struggled with the book work, the formulae and equations. To be honest, I've never been all that good with maths. Thank goodness computers do most of that for us now! I'm glad things worked out the way that they did, though. In high school, I did a psychology class and enjoyed it, but at university, I discovered all the breadth of the field of psychology, and I was hooked!

I never lost my interest in biology and medicine. Before I was ordained, I worked as a medical writer, writing journal papers and conference presentations based on the results of clinical trials of new drugs being developed. Over the years, although I've never done any formal study in it, I have developed an interest in the ethics surrounding advances in medicine and the challenges that medical science can bring. In fact, ethics is important to all of the sciences, because there will always be moral and social implications to the discoveries that science makes, the methods used to reach those discoveries and how those discoveries are used. This is one area in which I think Christianity can make a real contribution. After all, we've got 2,000 years' worth of experience in thinking about ethics relating to a variety of issues.

Currently, my field of study is the psychology of religion. Some might think that's a strange field for a Christian, and indeed a priest. But I don't study religion to debunk it. I study it so that I can understand it better and, I hope, share what I discover with others to benefit the wider church. Like other sciences, psychology can't prove or disprove the existence of God, because it doesn't study God. Psychology is the study of the way human beings think and feel and behave. Religion is a set of practices and activities undertaken in response to an awareness of the divine, and is a human activity. The way we go about it and the way our religious practices and beliefs shape our thinking and our behaviour is, therefore, a perfectly reasonable thing to study. Basically, studying the psychology of religion is just another way of helping us understand ourselves better, and I believe that can only be a good thing.

Of course, I still have an interest in other sciences, as well – especially anything to do with space (if anyone were to ask me now, I'd say my dream job would be being chaplain on the International Space Station). Astronomy is an amazing science. It's astounding how much we've been able to learn about worlds that are so far away. Equally astounding is what we can learn about our own world from things like comets and asteroids that we study in space. I also enjoy keeping up with the latest in physics and cosmology. I may not be able to understand the maths, but I do enjoy learning about the work that's being done in these fields, and the concepts and ideas that are behind that work. The breathtaking grandeur of the universe and the amazing complexity that lies in the smallest things at the heart of the physical world are both awe-inspiring. For me, that feeling of awe and wonder at the magnificent reality around us inevitably leads to a feeling of awe and wonder at the God who not only made it all, but loves and sustains it, and even chose to become a part of it.

7

Animals

 **Dr Andy Gosler** is University Research Lecturer in Ornithology and Conservation, and Director of the Ethno-ornithology World Archive (EWA) at Oxford University. He is one of the UK's most experienced ornithologists, teaching in the fields of ecology, evolution, conservation and ethnobiology. Having spent 30 years studying woodland birds, he has incorporated that experience into a research and teaching programme in ethno-ornithology: the study of birds and people. He is training for ministry in the Church of England and sees reconnecting people (and especially children) with nature as mission.

Introduction

Of all God's creation, animals are a bit special and, of course, even we are animals. All animals have their job to do and through the activities in this chapter we can learn more about the special job that God has created us to do: to look after the earth and each other, and to understand our place in the grand ecological scheme of things (Genesis 2:15; Genesis 6—9).

The world of the Bible is full of birds, fish and animals, unsurprisingly. We would expect domestic birds and animals (camels, sheep, doves, cattle, goats, chickens) to provide the background for an agricultural people, wild animals to be part of the landscape of those living much more closely to the planet than many of us do, and mythical animals to be part of a rich cultural heritage (Behemoth, Leviathan and dragons, for example). They feature significantly in the Old Testament stories of creation, Noah's ark, Balaam's donkey, Elijah and the ravens, many verses in Psalms (especially Psalm 148) and Proverbs, including memorably the ant (Proverbs 6), Jonah, Job and Isaiah's vision of the holy mountain.

Fish feature in several stories about Jesus – miraculous catches and the feeding of the 5,000 to name but two. He mentions birds several times, particularly in Matthew 6, comparing God's care of the 'birds of the air' to his care of human beings, or Luke 6 with his reference to sparrows for sale, or comparing his love for Jerusalem with that of a chicken for her chicks (Matthew 23). He sends demons into the pigs (Mark 5) and uses pigs to depict the utter depths to which the son in his parable has fallen (Luke 15). He uses the analogy of sheep and shepherds as a key image and the role of sacrificial lamb is significant throughout scripture. The donkey carries Jesus into Jerusalem and a cockerel crows to mark Peter's betrayal.

Acts 10 contains Peter's vision of the cloth full of animals and Revelation has the four strange creatures around God's throne which resemble animals (Revelation 4). The epistles (such as Romans 8) imply the presence of animals as part of God's creation.

Naming animals

Ratings

MESS 💡 💡 💡 💡 💡   DANGER 💡 💡 💡 💡 💡   DIFFICULTY 💡 💡 💡 💡 💡

Theme

Relationships

Equipment needed

Writing paper; graph paper; pens or pencils

Before you begin

In this experiment you are going to do a little social science to find out how many furry (mammals) or feathered (birds) animals people know, and whether or not they are better at naming local animals. In other animal experiments you'll have the chance to improve your knowledge of local animals of both these and other kinds.

Experimental method

Ask your participants to name 15 wild birds or mammals of any kind, and also to say whether they think the animal is found living in the British Isles. If they don't know what a mammal is, tell them it's an animal with fur. Write down the names in the order that they say them, together with whether they think they are found in the British Isles. You can record the person's name if they are happy to tell you, and also ask them their age in one of the categories below:

Age: 0–8; 9–14; 15–30; 30–50; older than 50.

These lists are data. If you have data, you are a scientist! Science is often about finding relationships in data and so here we want to know whether older people were better at naming local wild animals. A good way to see if there is a relationship is to plot a graph.

For each participant, plot a graph similar to the one below, in which the age group categories above are plotted against the number of animals that person knew. Was there a difference between older and younger people and were they more or less likely to name local animals? Don't worry if you don't get as far as plotting a graph; you'll have a lot of fun and interesting discussions while you conduct your social experiment.

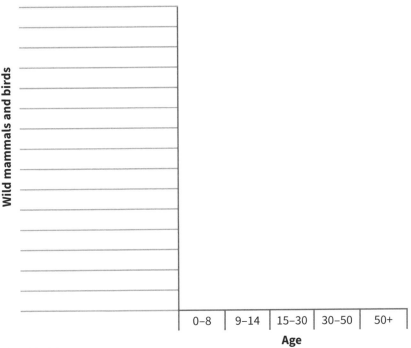

Big thinking

Naming is knowing and knowing is naming: it is difficult to know something without knowing its name because it is difficult to talk about it. People these days are often rather disconnected from nature. Before TV and the internet, everyone would have been able to tell you 15 British birds without much thinking about it, but today, well, how well did your people do? If you found that older people did better, it's probably because they learned these things when they were children, but why not ask them how they know and who taught them? You may find some surprises. People's ability to name creatures around them is a simple measure of their connectedness with nature. If you need to check if an animal that is named lives in the British Isles, use a phone or computer to do a quick check on the internet.

Big questions

Talk about the relationships people have with animals of all kinds, and why all creatures in God's creation, including us, are interdependent. Here are some thoughts to help you. In biblical times people lived much closer to the land, and so they knew the names of the plants and animals around them that they or their ancestors had given them. This is what Genesis 2:19–20 is talking about when it says: 'Now the Lord God had formed out of the ground all the wild animals and all the birds in the sky. He brought them to the man to see what he would name them; and whatever the man called each living creature, that was its name. So the man gave names to all the livestock, the birds in the sky and all the wild animals.' Through the previous verse (Genesis 2:18: 'The Lord God said, "It is not good for the man to be alone. I will make a helper suitable for him"'), this chapter is also telling us that it's important for people to understand that they need all the other creatures on earth to be fully human.

When did you last spend some time just messing about outside, looking at things in the park, garden or countryside?

Classification

Ratings

MESS 💡💡💡💡   DANGER 💡💡💡   DIFFICULTY 💡💡💡

Theme

Bringing order out of chaos

Equipment needed

Access to a pond; a wire coat-hanger; a bamboo garden cane; a pair of tights; a strong pair of pliers; duct tape; a few medium-large jamjars; a washing-up bowl in a light colour (yellow is ideal); drawing paper; pencils; a guide to pond life (optional); a magnifying glass of x10 or x20; a white saucer; a microscope (optional)

Before you begin

Animals are basically of two kinds: animals with backbones (called vertebrates), like us and our pets, including fish, amphibians, reptiles, birds and mammals; and animals without backbones (invertebrates) like snails, shrimps and water fleas, etc. In this experiment, you are going to either make a pond dipping net and collect some pond life to examine, or collect some pond water and examine it under a microscope. In both cases, see how many kinds you can distinguish – counting the legs is a good start. This is a starter programme for pond dipping and examining minibeasts, and you may also find these websites helpful: **www. gardensafari.net**, or **www.wildlifewatch.org.uk**.

Take care when working near water. Don't put yourself in a position where you might fall in, such as on a slope or slippery surface. Be sensible, but don't be afraid of the outdoors either.

Experimental method

To make a simple net for pond dipping, bend the coat-hanger into a square or diamond shape. Then tie the legs of the tights together in a tight knot where the thighs would be and cut off the remaining leg material. You now have a net. Place the net in the centre of the bent coat-hanger and fold the waistband over the wire, then sew a hem to keep it in place. With the pliers, bend the hook part of the hanger straight and either thread it into the end of the bamboo cane and secure with duct tape, or secure it to the outside end of the cane with duct tape. You now have a net to dip in your pond. Use the jamjars, washing-up bowl, saucer and microscope to examine your catch.

How many kinds of animals can you find? Return your catch to the pond after your work.

Big thinking

It is thought that there are about 8.7 million species (kinds) of plants and animals in the world, but only about 1.2 million have been named. It is reckoned that it would take 1,000 years to classify and name them all, but species are becoming extinct at such a rate because of human activity that it would be impossible even if we had that long.

Big questions

Whose planet is it? Think about Job 38, e.g. Job 38:4, where God asks Job: 'Where were you when I laid the earth's foundation? Tell me, if you understand.' We do not own the earth. We may lay claim to it, but it existed for billions of years before we even appeared and so we can only own it if its real owner gives it to us. But God has not given it to us to do with it what we want, because he loves his whole creation and he knows that we too have no future without all the creatures he created. Why are there so many kinds of plants and animals; what jobs are they doing? How does it change the way you shop, travel, eat, treat other people, plants and animals if you see the planet as not belonging to you?

Evolution: the grand adventure of life

Ratings

MESS DANGER DIFFICULTY

Theme

God creates creation to create itself

Equipment needed

Several sheets of A4 paper (or card for the evolution game as it will last longer); pens and pencils; coloured pencils; sticky tape or glue; scissors; three dice of different colours (make your own or use the templates online); pictures of animals (make your own or use the templates online)

Before you begin

In this exercise we are going to make one or two paper games that capture something of the wonder of evolution. One is a simple 'fortune teller' game, which might be more suitable for younger children, and the other a kind of board game for all ages. It's called 'The Evolution Game' or 'DICE AND MICE'.

Experimental method

You probably know how to play the fortune teller game. To make the game, find instructions online to fold the paper and write in the animals and questions as detailed below. There are lots of templates online.

Outer faces: write FROG, MOUSE, BIRD and SNAKE.

Inside: write the numbers one to eight.

Under flaps: write questions and answers. Here are some suggestions:

Q What is the unique feature of birds?
A Feathers are unique to birds.

Q When did mammals first appear on the earth?
A In the late Jurassic period about 200 million years ago.

Q What kind of animal is a frog, and what's special about them in animal history?
A They were the first vertebrates to occupy the land.

Q When did snakes first appear on the earth?
A Recently found fossils show snakes appeared at least 167 million years ago in the Jurassic period.

Q Name two ways mammals differ from birds.
A Lactation, hair, most have live young.

Q When did birds first appear on the earth?
A About 150 million years ago in the Jurassic period.

Q Most snakes and lizards lay eggs. What do we call snakes that have live young?
A They are called viviparous.

Q When did frogs evolve?
A The earliest frog fossils are from the Triassic period 145 million years ago.

To play the game: begin with the thumb and index fingers of each hand in the four pockets of the fortune teller. Have the person whose fortune is being read pick one of the animals on the top four flaps. If the animal is FROG, spell out the letters F-R-O-G while alternating pinching and pulling motions with the teller. Each pinch will expose four of the numbers on the inner flaps, and each pull will expose the other four numbers. After spelling out F-R-O-G, the teller will be showing one of the sets of four numbers. The other player will then pick one of those numbers, and you then continue alternating pinch and pull, like in the first round, except it continues with a counting of the number instead of the spelling of the animal. Once the number has been counted, four numbers will be exposed. After one is picked, ask the person the question under the flap and see how well they do.

The evolution game or, DICE and MICE
The object of the game is to construct a new animal using the parts (body, head, tail, front and rear limbs) of the animals depicted in the figures (download them online). You need three dice, or you can make them using the templates provided. Print and photocopy the animals, or draw your own, and cut them out. Also cut along the dotted lines to use the parts of each animal, and cut out the bird's wing.

Designate the yellow die to tell you what kind of animal to include in your evolving creature: 1 – snake, 2 – fish, 3 – frog, 4 – bird, 5 – mouse, 6 – your choice. The other two dice will tell you which parts to use, but you need both numbers the same to be able to include the parts in your animal as follows: double 1 – body; double 2 – head; double 3 – tail; double 4 – forelimbs; double 5 – hind limbs; 6 – free choice. You can use parts in any order but you must start with a body (1 or 6 on the yellow). And, yes, you can put wings on your snake's body, but the snake only contributes head, body and tail.

Big thinking

One thing that is special about humans is our big brains. God has given us the means to look around us and weigh the evidence of our own existence as a created thing – and God is who we have been able to discern as our creator. The biblical book of Genesis speaks of our origins. It tells us in the most wonderful and beautifully poetical form that God created us, out of the earth, but it doesn't tell us in detail how. Now, God has given us science to try to understand a bit more about how he did this, and it is clear that it was through the process of evolution. But we are still trying to understand how that works. Through the science of genetics, it is becoming clear that elements we thought rather random are actually less random than we thought, and that there are goals for evolution determined by what works and what doesn't in a process that Charles Darwin first recognised and called natural selection. So the evolution game has a rather random element – dice – shuffling genes, and a goal (a telos): you need to get the right numbers to win.

Big questions

Christians read the book of Genesis in different ways. Some say Genesis is a very special kind of poetry called allegory, which tells us some deep truths about our relationships with God and the rest of creation, but not in detail how he did it. So Genesis 2:19 says: 'Now the Lord God had formed out of the ground all the wild animals and all the birds in the sky,' and that he created us humans out of the earth – that is even what the name Adam means; we are of the earth. But creation is ongoing: as the Christian theologian Thomas Aquinas (1225–74) called it, Continuous Creation. So talk about how the book of Genesis captures in its first three chapters what you know about human origins from science, and how they are telling the same story in different ways and how, in an amazing way, charged with wisdom, and with our active participation, God has been 'playing the evolution game'.

Dinosaurs: God's grandeur

Ratings

MESS 💡💡 💡💡💡   DANGER 💡 💡💡💡💡   DIFFICULTY 💡💡 💡💡💡

Theme

Seeing things differently

Equipment needed

A large sheet of card, at least 1 m square; two square or rectangular compact travel mirrors; sticky tape or glue; scissors

Before you begin

Dinosaurs were the largest land animals ever to live on earth. Some of the herbivorous (plant eating) dinosaurs had very long necks so they could reach the tops of cycad trees to feed, and very long tails to counterbalance them so they didn't fall over. Their long necks meant that they would also have had an amazing view from up there! Carnivorous dinosaurs ate these massive herbivores, and so had to be massive also. So in this exercise, you will make a periscope to see the world from a different viewpoint.

Experimental method

Following the template online, estimate the dimensions to fit the mirrors available to you. Draw and cut out the shape of the periscope. Then fold along the internal lines and stick or glue the tabs to make a rectangular cylinder with a top and bottom and holes to insert the mirrors. Insert the mirrors at an angle so that each reflects into the other, and so when you look in one end of the periscope, you should be able to see the world through the other end.

Big thinking

Dinosaurs were a diverse group of warm-blooded animals that appeared on earth about 240 million years ago. They came to dominate the earth after a mass extinction event 200 million years ago that is recognised geologically as the boundary between the Triassic and Jurassic periods. They ranged in size from mice to the largest animals ever to walk on land, with examples such as the mighty brontosaurus, diplodocus and tyrannosaurus rex. The largest dinosaur was about 40 metres long. Dinosaurs persisted on earth for 160 million years, and left us some of the most exciting fossils. These revealed that some evolved to be able to fly (the pterosaurs), while others occupied the seas (the ichthyosaurs), becoming incredibly like the whales, which are mammals. The details of some of these fossils, revealing healed bones, suggest that carnivorous dinosaurs may even have cared for their own sick family members. Dinosaurs became extinct after another mass extinction event known as the Cretaceous/ Tertiary boundary 65 million years ago (so don't have nightmares!). One group of smaller dinosaurs evolved feathers, so that today we can recognise that, while most of the dinosaurs died out, the direct descendants of a few are birds!

Big questions

Sometimes it may be necessary for bad things to happen in order for better things to come into being. God sees this, because he sees and knows everything in absolute detail and wisdom, but that doesn't mean that he is always happy about what has to happen to bring about a good change. Think and talk about this in the context of the extinction of the dinosaurs, and of the crucifixion and how God suffers to bring about the necessary good (Jesus in Gethsemane: Matthew 26:36–46; who is Jesus praying to?).

Feed the birds

Ratings

MESS 💡💡💡 DANGER 💡💡💡 DIFFICULTY 💡💡💡

Theme

Hospitality

Equipment needed

Timber (treated plywood is good to use; where possible, use offcuts or wood waste as this is cheaper and saves waste); wooden post (if the table is to be freestanding; ideally 10x10 cm); saws; hammers; nails and/or screws of sufficient length to deal with whatever timber you have available (galvanised nails will last longer than plain steel nails); two or three screw-in cup hooks; bird feeder; bird feed (e.g. peanuts, black sunflower or niger seeds, sunflower hearts, etc.); a bird guidebook

Before you begin

In this exercise we'll build a simple bird table to feed the birds and stock it with appropriate food. Apart from being a lot of fun, think about what birds might come to the feeder, and what best to provide for them, especially in the winter when food is scarce.

Experimental method

Using the template provided online, draw out the design and cut out the pieces. Start with the table part itself, and nail on the edging strips so that there is a gap of about an inch in either direction at the corners. This provides a lip to stop food being knocked off the table by the birds, but the gap allows you to sweep the table clean when you need to. Next, nail or screw on the uprights, which support the roof and form the gable ends. (Note: the dimensions are not critical so long as it ends up looking something like the template online, and the roof fits.) The roof can also be nailed or screwed to the gable uprights, but if the table is to be attached to the post by a nail or two through the table, it may be wise to leave attaching the roof until last so that there is space for you to hammer through.

Alternatively, construct a square using blocks (E in template) on the underside of the table which can seat the whole table on to the post when it is in place. An alternative to using a post is to attach a couple of cup hooks to the ends of the roof and hang the table from a tree. This may have the disadvantage of being difficult to prevent squirrels from taking all the food. One or two cup hooks screwed into the edges of the table can act as fixings to hang additional feeders. Squirrel-proof feeders are available from many garden and household suppliers. Site your table where the birds have access to cover, and where you can watch and enjoy seeing the birds. Experiment with different foods and keep a diary of which birds visit your bird table. (See photos online.)

Big thinking

You may attract many different kinds of birds to your bird table. Robins will be early visitors, especially to the table itself. Tits will also visit the table, but will be more interested in hanging foods, especially peanuts and sunflower seeds. Blue tits, great tits and coal tits are likely visitors and, if you are lucky, maybe even a marsh tit or nuthatch. With hanging suet or fat balls you may attract long-tailed tits. Other visitors are likely to include various finches: chaffinch, greenfinch and goldfinch, and maybe even a siskin or great spotted woodpecker.

Big questions

In Matthew 10:29, Jesus tells his disciples that God even cares about the sparrows. God exists in intimate loving relationship with his creation, of which we are a part. If God loves his creation, shouldn't we? But we cannot love something we do not know, and a great way to start to know and love creation is to feed the birds in your churchyard and in your garden. Even people in high-rise flats have found ways to feed the birds. Many people find they understand God best by spending time with nature and trying to understand it. How do you think knowing God and knowing nature are linked so intimately that through knowing one, we can know the other?

Bees

Ratings

MESS   DANGER DIFFICULTY

Theme

Helping the homeless

Equipment needed

Blocks of rough timber, almost any width and about 15 cm long; drill with a selection of bits up to 1 cm width; a large tin or enough rough timber to make a box of any shape (see the sketch online); hammer; saws; nails; a magnifying glass

Before you begin

Do you know how important honey-bees are? They make honey and pollinate flowers so they can create seeds. But there are many other kinds of pollinators and some, such as bumble-bees and solitary bees, have become quite rare in recent years. So in this experiment, we are going to make a home for solitary bees. There are 240 kinds of these small bees in the UK, which, unlike honey-bees, place their eggs in individual compartments or nest cells rather than in a honeycomb that they have made from wax. They are also harmless, are not aggressive and don't sting. Some of the solitary bees are really small but nevertheless are important pollinators.

Experimental method

Drill a number of holes of different widths in the timber blocks and to the full depth of your bit. This will provide nest chambers for bees of different sizes. You can place the blocks in your tin as in the picture online, or make a 'hotel' for them which you can attach to the side of a shed, fence or wall or simply place on a wall; anywhere outdoors but reasonably sheltered. If they are around, the bees will find them.

You should try to manage your bee houses to prevent larvae dying in winter due to fungus moulds, and the spread of parasites. Ideally at the end of the summer try to identify any cells that remain 'walled-up' from the previous year because no young bees emerged. The contents of these cells will be dead and should be removed and destroyed. In summer, after the young bees have emerged, replace drilled blocks every couple of years. This helps to prevent the build-up of fungus moulds, mites and other pests and parasites. A magnifying glass will be helpful for inspecting the holes in your bee house to see if they are occupied.

Big thinking

So the plants need the bees for their pollination and the bees need the plants for the nectar for their larvae. They have evolved in a mutual dependency. We humans have also evolved in a mutual dependency with nature, but the problem is that, since we developed agriculture and came to live in towns and cities, it has become less obvious to many people that we are dependent on other creatures, and especially the millions of tiny pollinators that are essential if we want fruit. But we shouldn't help the bees just because we want something in return, but because it is the right thing to do. After all, we help others because it's the right thing to do, not because we expect something in return.

Big questions

The Bible has much to say about helping other people; for example the homeless. Look at the following passages from scripture: Isaiah 58:7; Leviticus 25:35–36; Proverbs 21:13; Matthew 25:34–40; Luke 10:25–37. Now talk about this in the context of helping all God's creatures, including humans, because Jesus says we cannot be trusted with big things if we can't be trusted with the little things (see Matthew 25:21).

Watching birds

Ratings

MESS  DANGER   DIFFICULTY

Theme

Observation as prayer

Equipment needed

Books about birds, mini-beasts, flowers, etc. to use as a reference; binoculars (with as high a magnification as possible; don't use opera glasses as they are not strong enough); notebooks; pencils

Before you begin

This is an exercise in watching. If you've made a bird table ('Feed the birds', p. 172), you are very well equipped for this. We have two big questions to ask: who is visiting, and where and on what are they feeding? If you do not have ready access to a garden to observe during Messy Church, perhaps you could video birds in a garden and then show the video as part of the Messy Church activity.

Experimental method

Sit yourself comfortably where you have a good view of the bird table, churchyard or garden and, using your binoculars to get a better view and your books to identify the birds coming, note down what species (kinds) are visiting, and how many of each there are. Also note the date and time and what they are feeding on. You can use the templates provided online to colour in and make notes if you like. Do birds of particular species visit alone or with other birds, and what species are present? Notice how the different birds have different kinds of beaks to feed on different kinds of foods. Now look beyond the bird table. What other birds are there and where are they feeding? Maybe a blackbird on the ground searching for earthworms (note especially where they forage as you may need that knowledge later), or a woodpecker in a tree, wrens in the undergrowth and the compost heap, robins perching watching the ground.

Where the birds feed, and what they eat, make up what is called their niche. The niche is the job the birds do, maybe keeping down the numbers of mini-beasts that, in the right numbers, are beneficial, but unchecked in this way might become pests and eat too much of the vegetation. You can do the birdwatching in summer or winter, but you may have more birds visiting the feeders in winter as natural food is scarcer then. If you do your watching at home, compare your notes with others back in church. Did you see the same kinds of birds?

Birds aren't the only creatures that have a niche. All plants and animals have their job to do. Watch the bees and wasps – they are busy collecting nectar to make honey for their larvae (babies), but at the same time they are pollinating the plants they visit so they can produce more plants. We encourage honey-bees to make enough honey for us, too. Which flowers do the bees especially like?

Big thinking

Good science starts with good observation: we want to understand the world around us. Many people don't really observe the world around them – they look, but do not see! So now you have some information on niches. Good observation has taught us that plants, animals, fungi and bacteria all work together in a way to create a community. Each species has its own job to do in that community, and together on a huge scale, since plants take up carbon dioxide and give out oxygen while animals breathe in oxygen and breathe out carbon dioxide, together they balance the amount of carbon dioxide in the atmosphere so even regulate the climate. The whole beautifully balanced self-regulating global system can't work if we cut down too many trees and cause plants and animals to go extinct.

If every species has a niche, what is the niche of humans?

Big questions

Jesus himself tells us to consider the birds of the air, and lilies of the field. In Romans 8:28, Paul tells us: 'We know that in all things God works for the good of those who love him, who have been called according to his purpose.' As God is the creator source of everything and Jesus is the creator God incarnated in human form, the very Lord of Life is the natural global expression of Paul's insight. The importance of observation and its link with prayer is suggested in Colossians 4:2, where Paul says, 'Devote yourselves to prayer, being watchful and thankful.' Talk about this in connection with what you have learned about nature and creation through your own observations.

'An inordinate fondness for beetles'

Ratings

MESS   DANGER   DIFFICULTY

Theme

All things work together for good

Equipment needed

Access to land, churchyard, glebe land, gardens, etc.; a book of mini-beasts as a guide; five plastic disposable cups; a small trowel; jamjars with lids

Before you begin

An eminent biologist, J.B.S. Haldane, was once asked what might we deduce about the creator from a study of nature. He replied, 'An inordinate fondness for beetles!' Why? About half of all the described living organisms in the world – that's plants, animals, fungi, bacteria, everything with the breath of life – and three-quarters of all described and named animals are insects, and nearly half of all insects are beetles! In this simple experiment, we are going to catch some mini-beasts and see how many kinds there are just crawling around the ground.

Experimental method

Dig a small hole, deep enough to set a plastic cup in and wide enough that it just fits snugly into the ground. It should look a bit like the hole in a golf or putting green. This is now a pitfall trap for mini-beasts. Set four more in the same way, at least five metres apart. Then leave them for a night. They could be set in place the day before Messy Church, so long as it's dry overnight. On your return, take up the cups, which will have caught anything small that wandered in and couldn't get out, and tip the contents into a small jamjar. Take the jars indoors to examine the contents. You might like to look at them under a microscope as described in 'Classification' on p. 165, but return the animals to where they came from afterwards.

As with 'Watching birds' (p. 176), if your Messy Church does not have access to a garden area, you could collect the beetles in a garden elsewhere and bring them in. But remember, please return them to the site where you collected them.

Big thinking

If you look carefully at your samples of mini-beasts, you will find that some are carnivorous (eat other creatures), like the centipedes, and some are herbivorous (eat plants), like the woodlice. If you count the number of herbivorous and carnivorous animals, you should find that there are far more herbivores than carnivores, and if you weighed them, the total weight of herbivores would surely be more than that of the carnivores.

Big questions

Talk about Genesis 1:24–25: 'And God said, "Let the land produce living creatures according to their kinds: the livestock, the creatures that move along the ground, and the wild animals, each according to its kind." And it was so. God made the wild animals according to their kinds, the livestock according to their kinds, and all the creatures that move along the ground according to their kinds. And God saw that it was good.'

So God has seen that it is good that there should be such a diversity of creatures and especially of mini-beasts. What do you think they are doing? What do you think they are there for? What might it tell us about how the living systems of the earth work that there are more herbivores than carnivores?

Worms, worms, worms

Ratings

MESS 🔆🔆🔆🔆   DANGER 🔆   DIFFICULTY 🔆🔆

Theme

Things aren't always what they seem

Equipment needed

A large, clean, glass jar with a screw top and holes punched in the lid so the worms can breathe; a trowel; some moist soil and sand; earthworms; plant matter such as dead leaves, vegetable peelings, tea leaves, some overripe fruit, etc.; some black paper; rubber bands; a cool dark cupboard; some newspapers

Before you begin

Here's a really messy fun one for you! We are going to make a wormery. So, you've been watching the blackbirds in the garden and discovered where they most like to forage. That's where the worms are. Alternatively, have a dig around the compost heap.

Experimental method

Cover your work surface with newspaper. Now put about 1 cm of sand at the bottom of the clean jar. Add a thick layer of soil, followed by a thin layer of sand and finally another thick layer of soil. You need to end up with about 5 cm of space at the top. Now, using what you learned by watching the blackbirds, go and dig up some earthworms. But before you add them to the jar, look closely at them. Can you tell which end is which? Can you guess how a worm moves? They use tiny hairs on the sides of their skin. Can you see them? Now put the worms in the jar and add some old leaves, vegetable peelings, tea leaves and the overripe fruit. Put the lid on – with a couple of holes punched in the lid so the worms can breathe – wrap black paper around the jar and put it into a cool, dark cupboard or box. Leave it for a couple of weeks and then observe what the worms are doing. Photograph or video this to show at your next Messy Church. What has happened to the vegetable peelings? What patterns did the worms make in the earth?

Big thinking

If you were to do this experiment in different kinds of soil, you'd discover that there are more worms in well-drained neutral or alkaline soils with some humus than in poorly-drained or waterlogged, acid soils with little humus. That's partly because those are the conditions worms like, but it's also the kind of soils worms create. They drag dead leaf litter down into the soil to feed on and they aerate the soil by their movements through it. So worms are really important for plants and everything else in soil because they improve soil fertility.

Big questions

Worms don't get a terrific press in the Bible (e.g. Mark 9:48) as they tend to be associated with death, corruption and decay, and represent the lowest forms of life – in fact, a comparison with humanity. But they are also essential to the great process of recycling, and so also representative of God's great wisdom in creation: that life creates the ideal conditions for its own existence. Talk about how worms help you to see the world differently, and how we might come closer to an appreciation of how God sees the world if we understood better the role of earthworms. Here's a clue – we might not like them, but they are a miracle gift to the world.

Nest boxes for birds

Ratings

MESS 🔆🔆🔆   DANGER 🔆🔆🔆   DIFFICULTY 🔆🔆🔆

Theme

Stewardship

Equipment needed

Rough-cut, unplaned, untreated softwood timber, 150 mm wide x 1500 mm long x 15 mm thick (where possible use offcuts or wood waste as this is far cheaper and reduces waste); scrap rubber, such as an old inner tube from a tyre to form a hinge; galvanised 20 mm nails; saws; hammers; hand brace or drill (with 28 mm-diameter bit); pencil; ruler; a little wire and a screw eye; scissors; a book on birds for reference

Before you begin

God loves his creation, of which we are a part, and as a parent loves to see her children being good to each other, so God delights in our caring for creation. So in this exercise we are going to show some hospitality to nature and make two nest boxes. Because of human actions, spotted flycatchers have declined greatly in numbers in the UK over the last 50 years and are now endangered. But they love to nest in churchyards. So make an open-fronted nest box for them and site it in ivy on a tree or wall in the churchyard. Because of their scarcity, you may be lucky to have it used, so make a second box for tits and you can enjoy watching them. If spotted flycatchers do use your open-fronted box, please report it to your local bird club.

Experimental method

You can make a nest box out of a single plank of wood (details above), measured and cut according to the template provided online. We think the principles should be fairly obvious for you to nail this together, recognising that you have a roof and a floor, front, back and sides. Attach the piece of rubber as a hinge between the back and the roof so that the roof can be lifted for inspection, and screw the eye into the side of the roof about an inch from the front and attach the wire to hook around it. This can act as a lock to secure the roof against predators and strong wind. Site both kinds of box in cover on a wall or tree, never in direct sun where the chicks can overheat, or facing west where the rain will come in, and place it out of reach of cats, too. (See photos online.)

Big thinking

Science is ultimately all about doing our job of looking after the earth better, and God's wisdom is seen in the joy of discovery, of finding out how, and even why, things work – of being given the privilege of thinking God's thoughts after him. In this series of activities, we discovered that every animal has its own job to do, and we thought about our job, our niche. The more you think about the human purpose in this amazing creation, the more it does seem that our role is to look after and safeguard the whole system, which works through the interaction of thousands of different species channelling a tiny part of the sun's energy through plants and animals and even regulating the climate.

Big questions

Talk about the creation story in the Bible and how, using poetic imagery, it captures the essence of our essential God-given purpose. (Genesis 2:15: 'The Lord God took the man and put him in the Garden of Eden to work it and take care of it.') The very fact that it is poetry helps it to carry the wisdom to understand the human story and our place in the world. Think about how the text shows order coming out of chaos, and how science reveals the exquisite beauty, the mathematical perfection, of that order. We are creatures, not gods, and we are as dependent as all other creatures on the life-giving energy of the sun, water, the rotation of the earth and the moon to regulate the tides, on all other creatures that together make life possible, and crucially and ultimately on God's wisdom and loving oversight of all. Romans 12:13: 'Share with the Lord's people who are in need. Practise hospitality.'

Perspective

Lesley Gray has a PhD in biochemistry and DNA and teaches science at secondary level.

I have always had a fascination with the world around me. As a small child, this started in my back garden digging for worms and grew to Tipo the goat, whom I hand-reared one summer holiday on a farm. I very quickly became interested in science and the things it could tell me about the world, but I always felt that it did not give me all of the answers. I started searching elsewhere for the answers to bigger questions; the God whom I heard about in lessons at school seemed to be a possible source. At the age of twelve I made the decision to begin going to church. I took myself, every Sunday, to a small local church not too far from my house, and it was here my journey of faith began.

Throughout my teenage years my quest continued. I learned more about God, the creator, at church and more about the incredible world we live in, at school. I did not see many conflicts between the two, but I also kept the two fairly separate in my own life. I seemed naturally to excel in my biology and chemistry lessons and so the obvious progression for me was into a degree in biochemistry at the University of Surrey. It was not until the third year of my course, when I was on an industrial placement year at the National Institute for Medical Research in London, that I truly began to understand what science is all about; it is not memorising information from textbooks, but it is discovering something new, in areas previously untouched. On completion of my degree, the natural progression for me was to begin a research PhD, in the same laboratory as my placement year.

My PhD involved looking at the process of rolling circle replication; this is how bacteria transfer their antibiotic-resistant DNA, resulting in us not getting better, even with the antibiotics doctors give us. This is something which only now is getting the media attention it deserves; with things like death from MRSA being reported in the news. For me, studying DNA, my Christian faith is really important, as it is my way of looking at how God has made us. Doing scientific research is a way of worshipping God; it is my way of saying to him that I am so amazed by his creation that I want to find out more about it.

DNA, in its most basic form, is a series of letters, and these letters put together give different codes, which our bodies use to make proteins, and we are essentially a big bag of proteins. DNA is very similar to the codes which are used to make computer programs. Computer programs do not create themselves, but have a very clever computer programmer writing them. In my view DNA is the same: a very intricate code, which could not have written itself to work in the amazing, life-giving ways it does without a programmer behind it: God!

During my scientific research I also had a very personal journey with science and faith. At the age of 21 I was diagnosed with Hodgkin's Lymphoma, a blood cancer. In fact, I used my own scientific understanding to diagnose myself four months before any doctor did! My studies meant that I could understand what the cancer was doing in my body and I also had a complex knowledge of how the chemotherapy drugs were helping to save my life. As a scientist, I could not really refuse being part of a clinical trial and was pleased to find out that, six years on, the trial treatment is now the standard and improved treatment for cancer patients. However, my scientific understanding of cancer could not answer the bigger questions: 'Why me?', 'What now?', 'How do I use this for good?' While science could tell me I had a 50 per cent chance of surviving for five years post-treatment, only God can explain why I have made it. For me, this was the ultimate mix of science and faith in my life, an experience which I carry with me every day of my life.

At the end of my PhD, I had a decision to make about my future. While science for me is a way of worshipping God, I sensed that he was calling me in a different direction. During my PhD I had volunteered at weekend youth residentials, with Youth for Christ. We asked the young people what was holding them back from God; my heart was saddened when I saw one person write, 'Science teachers and lessons at school'. The same weekend, I met a young man who was very excited to spend time with a scientist who was a Christian. He thought that, because of his faith, he would be excluded from a career in science. It was these encounters which led me to train as a science teacher. I am now in my second year of teaching science to secondary school students. While I may not be worshipping God by discovering something new, I am instead trying to inspire the future generation. It surprises me how regularly questions of science and faith pop up in the classroom, with students of all religious backgrounds. The very nature of science is to ask questions and we as Christians should be asking questions and helping others to do so, whether we know the answers right now, or not.

8

Power and energy

Paul Osborne BSc (Hons) PGDip is enthusiastic about bridging the perceived gap between science and faith. A professsional chemist with over 20 years' experience and a lifelong Christian, he is passionate about encouraging children to question everything, including science and faith. He is a father of one who has tested this passion to the limit with 'why?' questions!

With additional material by **David Gregory** and **Lucy Moore**.

Introduction

We come across power and energy every day, but maybe we don't always realise it. If you are watching what you eat and counting calories, then you are watching how much energy you take into your body – calories are an old-fashioned measure of energy. And when you flip a light switch, you are using electrical energy to make lights come on in your home.

In this series of activities, we will be looking at different kinds of energy, how they can be turned from one kind to another and how we can use energy to make things happen.

In the Bible, God himself is described as a God of power, both in the sense of having authority and in the sense of 'being able' to make things happen, especially in the Psalms (such as 68 and 89) but also in many other books: power is understood to be part of who God is. There are many stories in which people are given the power to do something beyond what they would humanly be able to do or want to do: Old Testament examples include Samson, David, Elijah and Gideon. Isaiah prophesied that people who wait on God will receive power and energy (Isaiah 40: 29–31). The powerless are seen as having a special place in

God's heart and plans (such as Psalm 72). And less benevolent bodies are also seen as having power, like Daniel's vision in Daniel 7:7 or death itself in Hosea 13:14.

Gospel stories about power include any account of Jesus' miracles, including the healing of the woman who touched him in Mark 5:30 when Jesus 'realised that power had gone out of him'. He also seems to share his power with his disciples, such as Peter being able to walk on water, or when his disciples find they can do miracles in Jesus' name.

Perhaps the most significant outpourings of power come at Jesus' resurrection and in the coming of the Holy Spirit in Acts 2. Power and weakness echo through the epistles too, and power is renamed as an attribute of God throughout Revelation in the acclamations of heavenly praise.

Make a milk carton car

Ratings

MESS 🔆🔆🔆🔆🔆   DANGER 🔆🔆🔆🔆🔆   DIFFICULTY 🔆🔆🔆🔆🔆

Theme

Energy and movement

Equipment needed

An empty 300 ml milk carton (or smallish cereal box); four plastic milk carton lids; sticky tape; bamboo skewers; two plastic drinking straws; scissors; metal skewer (to punch holes in your wheels); balloon; craft glue (optional)

Experimental method

Your bamboo skewers (axles) need to be long enough to go across the base of the milk carton (or box) and fit into two plastic lid wheels on either side. So line up the two wheels on either side of the carton and cut two pieces of bamboo skewer that will fit.

Take one of the straws and cut it into two pieces, slightly shorter than the width of the milk carton/cereal box's base. Thread your bamboo skewer axles into each straw.

Make holes in the centre of each plastic lid wheel. The easiest way to do this is for an adult to heat the tip of a metal skewer and then use it to melt a hole through the centre of each plastic lid. Put your plastic wheels on to your axles. Make sure they're nice and snug. If you like, you can put a dab of craft glue on to keep them secure.

Tape the straw axles to the base of the milk carton (make sure they are far enough apart that the wheels can move without hitting each other). Take the second straw and, using the sticky tape, attach it to the open end of the balloon, making an airproof seal using more sticky tape. Attach the straw to the top of the carton, so that the end sticks off the end of the carton by 5 cm. Blow the balloon up a bit (not too much or your milk-mobile will be toppled over by the force). Let it go and watch it shoot across the floor.

You might need to do a bit of trial and error to work out how much force the car needs to just trundle along rather than be blown over. This will be a good learning activity on the nature of forces.

Big thinking

The balloon-powered car is an example of turning 'potential' energy into 'kinetic' energy, the energy of motion.

When you blow up the balloon, the expanding elastic material the balloon is made of stores the energy that your body uses when it blows air into the balloon. The energy stored in the balloon is called potential energy. When you let the balloon go, this stored energy is converted to kinetic energy as the air pushes out of the balloon.

Nearly 400 years ago, the scientist Isaac Newton described rules – which scientists call laws – to describe how things move. Newton's third law says that for every action, there is an equal but opposite reaction. For example, if you push something, then it pushes you back. So, as the air pushes out of the balloon, the carton the balloon is attached to gets pushed in the opposite direction and moves forward.

You might want to ask: what would make the car go faster – a bigger or smaller balloon? What about if you used a bigger or smaller straw?

Big questions

What 'makes us move' as human beings? What gives us the motivation to do things – maybe amazing things? This activity had energy from the air in the balloon, but what sort of energy makes us help other people, make the world a better place, do extraordinary things for friends or strangers? How would you say 'love' is the same as energy? How do you think God's Holy Spirit, sometimes known as his 'breath', moves us?

Water power

Ratings

MESS 🐱🐱🐱🐱 DANGER 🐱🐱🐱🐱🐱 DIFFICULTY 🐱🐱🐱🐱🐱

Theme

The power of water

Equipment needed

500 ml plastic bottle; skewer; pencil; two bendable straws; blu-tack; string; water; bowl or bucket

Experimental method

Make two holes approximately 5 cm above the base of the bottle with the skewer and pencil, just large enough for the straws to fit through. Try to get these as even as you can. Cut the two straws, 2 cm each side of the bendy part. Insert one end into the holes in the bottle, bending them so they face opposite directions. You may need to use the blu-tack to make a waterproof seal where the straw goes into the bottle.

Use the string to make a harness around the top of the bottle, so the bottle is free to swing when it is held up. The easiest way to do this is to tie two pieces of string around the top of the bottle, and then tie them together about 10 cm above the top of the bottle.

Fill the bottle with water, and hold up above the bowl or bucket so that it spins.

Big thinking

As the water pours out of the two straws, the bottle should start to rotate. This is again an example of the conversion of potential (stored) energy to kinetic (movement) energy and Newton's third law of motion (see 'Make a milk carton car' on p. 188).

The water in the bottle stores energy, which is changed to motion energy as the water is drawn out of the straws by gravity. Shooting out of the straws in opposite directions, it makes the bottle start to spin.

Watch what happens as the level of water drops in the bottle – does the bottle spin slower or faster? It should spin slower because as the water level drops there is less stored energy to be converted to kinetic energy in the moving water.

What happens if you straighten the straws? Or have them facing in opposite directions? Or if you add two more straws to let the water flow out?

Big questions

The water has energy because of gravity pulling it downwards. Jesus said, 'Whoever believes in me, as scripture has said, rivers of living water will flow from within them' (John 7:38). Do you think you get more energy when you serve God and other people (in other words, when the living water is pouring *out of* you) or when you're listening to God's word (in other words, when the living water is being poured *into* you)? Is it the same for everyone, do you think?

Balloon rocket

Ratings

MESS   DANGER   DIFFICULTY

Theme

The power of wind

Equipment needed

Balloon; long piece of string (about 3 m); drinking straw; sticky tape; two stick-on hooks (optional)

Experimental method

Thread the string through the straw and then suspend it so that it is taut across the room or between two stepladders or chairs. The experiment will work best if one end is higher than the other. The straw needs to be able to move freely along the string.

Using the sticky tape, attach the balloon to the straw, making sure you are still able to blow it up. Blow up the balloon but don't tie it off, just hold it pinched shut.

Move the straw to the high end of the string and let go – watch your balloon rocket fly along the string. You could turn this into a race if you like, timing how long each rocket takes to get from one end of the string to the other, and marking up scores.

Tip: If the straw sticks on the string, wipe the string with some furniture polish to make it slippery.

Big thinking

If you have made the balloon-powered car (see p. 188) and explained how that works, you might want to ask people how they think the rocket balloon works. It is the same principle as explained there; potential (stored) energy is converted to kinetic (motion) energy of the air pushed out of the balloon. The force exerted by the expelled air is called 'thrust'. It causes the straw to travel along the string due to Newton's third law of motion.

This is the same way a rocket works. There, thrust is made by burning fuel to make hot gases which are pushed out of the bottom of the rocket, making it travel up into space.

Big questions

In this activity, the balloon keeps needing to be blown up again to keep it moving. How do we get our energy for living God's way? Do you ever feel like the empty balloon? Do you ever feel like the full balloon? Many people following Jesus need to keep on being filled up by praying and reading the Bible as well as other ways. I wonder which ways you find helpful to keep on being filled with energy?

Speedboat matchsticks

Ratings

MESS 💡💡💡 💡💡   DANGER 💡 💡💡💡   DIFFICULTY 💡💡 💡💡

Theme

The energy of water; floating on water

Equipment needed

Water; bowl or shallow plate; washing-up liquid; cotton bud; spent matchsticks; ground black pepper (optional)

Experimental method

Fill a bowl with water and float a matchstick on the water in the centre of the bowl. Place a small amount of washing-up liquid on one end of the cotton bud, leaving the other end dry.

With the dry end of the stick, touch the water just behind the match. Watch what happens. Now, use the end with washing-up liquid on to touch the water just behind the match. Watch what happens. The match should shoot across the water like a power point. How many times can you make it do this?

You could do this experiment in a large tray of water, dropping in lots of matchsticks, and get each participant to experiment with moving the matchsticks themselves.

Optional: Dispose of the water, and wash the bowl to ensure no washing-up liquid remains. Then refill with water and sprinkle ground black pepper on so the surface is covered. Now touch the centre of the water with the cotton bud with washing-up liquid on. What happens? (The black pepper should shoot away to the edge of the bowl.)

Big thinking

Water molecules are like a battery – they have a positively and a negatively charged end. The electric charges attract one another and make the water stick together. But at the surface, the water does not stick to the air above, so they pull towards one another more. This is called surface tension and it means that small, light objects can float on water.

Adding washing-up liquid pushed the water molecules at the surface apart, which pushes the boat along. The same thing happens with the ground pepper – it gets pushed to the edge of the bowl. Why does the pepper move farther and faster than the matchstick when you touch the water with the cotton bud? Perhaps because the individual particles are lighter?

You can see water tension in a glass – just look at where the water touches the edge: it is slightly higher than the level of water in the glass. Or pour water on to a water-resistant surface. The water clumps together in drops because of the energy of surface tension. And on a pond, some insects like 'water boatmen' can walk on water because surface tension holds them up.

Big questions

Look at the story of Jesus and the children in Matthew 19:13–14. The disciples tried to push the children away, but Jesus kept on drawing them back. Have you ever known a time when you felt pushed away from Jesus? Or from someone else? How might you be more like the surface tension of the water and bring people together? Jesus calls this being a 'peacemaker' – it's a very valuable part to play at home, at school, at work, in politics…

Static electricity

Ratings

MESS   DANGER   DIFFICULTY

Theme

Changes of energy; static electricity

Equipment needed

A dark room; low-energy light bulb (fluorescent tube type); balloon

Experimental method

You will need a darkened room for this experiment. Blow up the balloon and rub it against your hair 10–20 times. Pass the balloon back and forth over the glass end of the light bulb – you should see the bulb glow faintly.

Optional: What happens if you put the balloon next to someone's hair? Does this new hairstyle suit them?

Big thinking

The friction between the balloon and your hair pulls small particles called electrons from the atoms of the balloon material. Electrons have a negative charge – electricity is made up of a flow of electrons. In this case, they stick to the surface of the balloon and give it a negative charge. This is called static electricity.

When you move the charged balloon over the bulb, this attracts positively charged particles in the gas inside the bulb – made of neon and mercury – towards the negatively charged balloon. As they move through the gas, this causes ultraviolet light (the same light that will give you a suntan or burn) to be emitted, which causes the wall of the light bulb to glow.

This experiment is an example of how energy changes from one form to another. Moving the balloon on your hair uses mechanical energy as your arm moves back and forth. This generates electrical energy in the balloon, which then makes light energy in the bulb.

Big questions

What sort of energy do we pass on to people around us? Are we positive people or negative people? What sort of energy did Jesus have? How did he change people when he came close to them? Can you think of anyone who changed when they came close to Jesus?

Bottle rocket

Ratings

MESS   DANGER   DIFFICULTY

Theme

Explosive power

Equipment needed

Safety glasses; newspaper and paper towels; plastic washing-up bowl; antacid (such as Alka-Seltzer) or denture cleaning tablets; a small plastic bottle with a snap-on lid (those from probiotic drinks such as Benecol work well); blu-tack; water; vegetable oil (optional), cola (optional)

IMPORTANT: This experiment requires you to wear protective safety glasses.

Experimental method

Put on your safety glasses. Place the newspaper on the table and floor, and the plastic washing-up bowl on to it. Take the antacid or denture cleaning tablet and stick it to the inside of the lid of the bottle using blu-tack.

Fill the bottle two-thirds full with water and then fix the lid on the bottle, making sure the tablet does not fall in! Turn the bottle upside down so the water falls on to the tablet, and place it lid-down in the bowl.

Now wait! Time how long it takes for the explosion to take place – the bottle should fly off the lid like a rocket!

Optional: Try this experiment with a different liquid, like vegetable oil or cola. Does it take a longer or shorter amount of time? Or try with a different amount of fluid. Does it take a different time if you use cold or warm (but not boiling) water?

Big thinking

There is a chemical in the tablet called sodium bicarbonate. This reacts with water to release the gas carbon dioxide. If you drop one of the tablets into a glass of water you can see the gas fizzing off.

In the sealed bottle, the gas builds up, and the pressure inside the bottle begins to increase. If you dare, you can feel the bottle get harder to squeeze as time goes on. The pressure keeps on building until the force it puts on the lid causes the bottle to fly off!

Try the optional activities above. Change only one thing about the experiment at a time. Scientists call this changing the variable, and it enables them to explore the different factors that can change the result of the experiment.

Did the bottle rocket launch if you used oil? Try dropping a tablet into a glass of oil – does it fizz? How does this explain what you saw when you used oil inside the bottle? (Oil does not react with the sodium bicarbonate so does not produce carbon dioxide.)

Big questions

Sometimes feeling as if we're fizzing and bubbling is about being excited. What makes you fizz and bubble? Is it okay if it's different from what makes someone else fizz and bubble? (Wouldn't it be boring if we were all the same!) Sometimes we feel like these bottles, with pressure slowly building up inside us and making us more and more angry: we want to explode like the bottles do! The Bible says a fruit of the Spirit is 'self-control' (Galatians 5:23). What methods are you learning to become more self-controlled when you feel this angry?

Penny battery

Ratings

MESS   DANGER   DIFFICULTY

Theme

Power from ordinary things

Equipment needed

A bowl of vinegar; ten copper coins, either 1p or 2p; ten pieces of aluminium foil, cut to the same size as the coins; 20 strips of paper, cut to the same size as the coins; a test subject; an LED light (you may be able to extract one from a light that is broken or they can be purchased on the internet quite cheaply); two pieces of plastic-coated wire (10 cm in length); multi-meter (optional)

Experimental method

Soak the strips of paper in the vinegar. Take one of the copper coins and place on a flat surface – you may want to lay it on some kitchen paper. Place a piece of the vinegar-soaked paper on top of the coin.

Next, place a piece of the aluminium foil on top of the paper. This makes one 'cell' of the battery. If you have a multi-meter, place the electrodes on the copper coin and the aluminium foil. Does it register a voltage?

Then, place a copper coin on top of the foil, followed by a piece of paper and then a piece of aluminium foil. Repeat until you have used up all the coins. You could retest at each layer to see if the voltage produced increases as you add more 'cells'.

Remove the plastic coating from the end of the wire. Attach the two wires to the leads of the LED light, and then hold the other ends of the wires to the top and bottom of the pile of coins. What do you see? Alternatively, moisten your fingers with a little of the vinegar, and then pick up the battery carefully using two fingers. What do you feel?

Big thinking

You just made a wet cell battery, the first type of battery made 200 years ago by Alessandro Volta. 'Volt', the unit of electrical potential which is how we measure the strength of a battery to produce electricity, is named after him.

The battery contains two metals – copper and aluminium – that release small particles called electrons at different rates when they react with the acid in the vinegar – called the electrolyte. The aluminium releases more electrons than the copper, and these move to the copper. The flow of electrons through the metal and wire is called an electric current.

There should be sufficient electricity produced to light up the LED bulb. Or, for those of you who like a bit more risk, to give you a tingling sensation when you hold the battery in your hands – a small electric shock!

Can you think of any things that have batteries in them? Most will work like the 'wet' cell, but will use dry material for the electrolyte between the metal plates as it's less messy to carry around.

Big questions

How amazing that power is all around us: we just need the right things in the right order in the right way to make it flow! Think about whether you might be just the right person at just the right time in just the right place for God's power to flow through you – maybe to help someone who needs it, or to heal a broken situation or bring God's love there. Think of people in the Bible who were the right people at the right time in the right place – people like Esther, or Naaman's slave girl.

Coin tower

Ratings

MESS   DANGER   DIFFICULTY

Theme

Staying balanced; moving with God

Equipment needed

A pile of coins; butter knife or similar blunt knife

Experimental method

Stack the coins into an even and straight tower. Sliding the butter knife to hit the bottom coin, try to knock it out from under the tower without it falling over.

Vary the speed at which you hit the coin. What happens when the knife is moving slowly and then very fast?

If you manage to hit the lowest coin fast enough, you should be able to knock it away without the tower toppling over. How many coins you can swipe out before the tower topples?

Big thinking

There are different forces at work in this experiment. To understand them you need to understand a law (or rule) that Isaac Newton figured out 400 years ago – his first law of motion. This says that unless something happens to an object from the outside, it stays still or keeps on moving in the same direction.

In the case of the pile of coins, once stacked, only the force of gravity pulls on them in a downward direction and, supported by the table or floor, they stay still. When the knife hits the bottom coin, this force causes it to move in a horizontal direction.

There is another force too – friction between the coins. You can feel friction: try rubbing your fingers along a table or rough surface. The rubbing together of the two surfaces makes it harder to move your fingers.

When you hit the bottom coin out of the way, there is friction between it and the coin above. If you do this slowly, the friction causes the coin above the one you hit to move too, which makes the tower topple. But if you hit the lowest coin with the right amount of speed, the force you use makes the coin move so fast that friction does not have enough time to make the next coin begin to move and the tower drops, almost perfectly, into the spot where it was before.

Big questions

How do we stay balanced when so many things try to topple us over or push us in ways that aren't God's ways? People who follow Jesus need to work hard to find their 'resting place' in Jesus: they practise every day. Ask someone here what they do to stay resting (or moving) in Jesus.

Insulation

Ratings

MESS 💡💡 💡💡💡   DANGER 💡 💡💡💡💡   DIFFICULTY 💡 💡💡💡💡

Theme

Flow of energy

Equipment needed

A rubber glove; a leather glove; a woollen glove; an insulated glove (like a 3M Thinsulate glove); a few bags of frozen peas

Experimental method

Place the bags of peas into people's hands. They should feel the cold of the peas straight away. Then place each glove on in turn and hold the peas. Time how long it takes for people to feel the cold of the peas on their hands. Which material protects people from the cold the longest time?

Big thinking

Heat energy – measured by temperature – is due to the atoms of a substance vibrating. The more heat energy the substance has, the more they vibrate. Heat flows from hot to cold, as the vibration of the atoms in the hotter substance causes those of the cold substance to vibrate more as they come into contact. This process is called heat conduction.

When you place the cold peas into your hands, heat energy from your warm hands flows from them to the frozen peas. Heat energy always flows from hot things to cold things. Although your hand gets cold, no energy is lost as the peas warm up by the same amount of energy. This is called the conservation of energy.

Materials that are insulators stop this flow of heat energy. Their atoms do not vibrate as quickly when they are brought into contact with a warm object, or they trap heat within them by storing heat inside small pockets of air which cannot come into contact with the cold peas. Your hand is still losing heat to the cold peas, but not as quickly as your body makes heat from the food you eat.

Big questions

These gloves protect our hands – some are better at it than others. What sort of protection do you think Paul means when he writes: 'Therefore put on the full armour of God, so that when the day of evil comes, you may be able to stand your ground, and after you have done everything, to stand' (Ephesians 6:13)? Why does the Lord's Prayer include the line 'Lead us not into temptation but deliver us from evil'? What do you think is a more fierce attack: negative things in social media, unhelpful images of people in films, friends who say nasty things, people who tempt us to do the wrong thing? How often should we pray for protection?

Greenhouse effect

Ratings

MESS 💡 💡 💡 💡 💡   DANGER 💡 💡 💡 💡 💡   DIFFICULTY 💡 💡 💡 💡 💡

Theme

Climate change

Equipment needed

Two 2-litre plastic bottles; cold water; Alka-Seltzer tablets or similar; blu-tack; two glass or electronic thermometers; bright lamp or a place where there is strong sunlight

Experimental method

Note: This experiment may take 30–60 minutes, so you may want to run it as a demonstration through the time of your Messy Church, setting it up at the beginning and then checking on the result at the end.

Take the two bottles and pour in equal amounts of cold water, around 5–8 cm deep. Take the lids off the bottles and make holes in the top large enough for the thermometers to fit through. Secure them in place by sealing the hole around them with the blu-tack. Place the lids with the thermometers on to the bottles. The bottom of the thermometer should be in the air towards the top half of the bottle, not in the water. Take a note of the temperature of each – they should be the same. You may need to leave them for a few moments to let them settle down.

Take an Alka-Seltzer tablet and drop it into one of the bottles, quickly sealing it with the lid. You will see the tablet fizzing, releasing a gas called carbon dioxide into the bottle.

Put both of the bottles in a sunny place or in front of a bright light. You will need to leave them for 30–60 minutes. You might want to check over time what is happening to the temperature of the bottles.

After an hour, which bottle is warmer?

Big thinking

The bright light heats the air and water in the bottle, proving the same amount of heat energy to each. In the bottle in which Alka-Seltzer is added, extra carbon dioxide is added to the air. This is a so-called greenhouse gas which traps heat energy more powerfully than the other gases in air – mainly nitrogen and oxygen. Because there is more of it in the air above the water in one bottle, this warms up faster and after an hour the thermometer shows a higher temperature.

In the earth's air there is only a very small amount of carbon dioxide. To give you some idea, take ten people and get them to sit in a circle. Get two of them to stand. They represent the amount of oxygen in air, the gas that we need to live – get them to breathe in and out just to remind them that we use oxygen when we breathe. Ask another seven people to stand – they represent the amount of nitrogen in the air. Plants need nitrogen to be healthy – get them to raise their arms in the air and wave them about like trees blowing in the breeze! Ask the final person to stand. They too are mostly made up of oxygen and nitrogen. But their feet represent the water vapour in the atmosphere, another greenhouse gas which helps warm the earth. And their toes represent the small amount of carbon dioxide in the air. But even though it is small it is powerful. This small amount warms the earth by 15 degrees centigrade, turning it from what would have been an ice ball to one where it is warm enough for life to live. When it gets warm, it begins to move around. And when it moves around, all the other gases move with it! Why not get the 'carbon dioxide' person to start a Mexican wave and let it go around the circle to help people remember that greenhouse gases warm the planet?

We make most of our energy from fossil fuels – coal, oil, gas – that are the remains of plants and animals from millions of years ago. When we burn them they produce carbon dioxide; over the past 200 years the amount in the atmosphere has increased by almost a half and the earth's temperature has risen by a degree. Weather patterns are starting to change, and if we keep on adding carbon dioxide at the same rate, the temperature will increase even more, making some regions very difficult for people to live in, and destroying lots of plants and animals.

Big questions

You can read the first few chapters of Genesis as a beautiful poem about God making the earth and how he feels about it. What do you think he might feel about greenhouse gases changing the world he made, hurting animals and people? How might we make a difference?

Perspective

Hannah Earnshaw is a PhD student at Durham, studying astrophysics, and is on the shortlist for the one-way mission trip to Mars.

I've always loved finding out how things work – whether it be the cut-away diagrams and models which let you look inside a piece of machinery and figure out which bits make other bits move, or an equation which very simply describes a very complicated-seeming phenomenon. One of my favourite experiences is that 'light-bulb moment' when all of a sudden something that I didn't understand before now makes perfect sense, and I can see the world in a new light. At school, the class that did that for me was physics, and it was one of my favourite subjects.

I get a great sense of awe and wonder simply by looking up at a clear night sky. I wanted to know more about everything out there in space – all those stars and planets that I could see, and everything further beyond them that I couldn't see, and most importantly how it all worked! That's why I went on to study physics at university, and then continued into a PhD in astronomy. And now my day job is to analyse X-rays from beyond our galaxy to learn more about how black holes work, some of the most extreme and alien objects in existence. It's hard to find somewhere in the universe that is less like our earth than the roiling, twisted space around a black hole filled with hot and brightly glowing gas, and yet it follows the same laws of physics that apply here on earth.

But learning new things about the world is not just exciting for its own sake: getting to know creation provides us with insight into the one who created it. For example, take the laws of physics. We observe them to be the same wherever we look in the universe – everything, everywhere, following the same rules. This tells me of a God who is constant, not arbitrary, a God who plans and designs rather than doing things at random. And yet the amount of variety that these same laws generate is stunning, like the unique nature of each planet in our solar system, and the planets around other stars that are completely different again. And this tells me of God's boundless imagination and creative genius, that he made a universe that follows rules we are capable of discovering and comprehending, but which allows for asteroids and comets, nebulae and supernovae, spiral galaxies and elliptical galaxies, red dwarfs and blue supergiants, black holes and neutron stars – and a beautiful planet full of all sorts of life which is our wonderful home.

The sheer scale of the universe tells me some challenging things about God as well. That the universe is billions of years old, and that all that time passed before humans even came into being, tells me that God is ancient and patient, and that his timing may not always be comprehensible to us. That we live on a tiny planet around a nondescript star in one galaxy out of billions in the vastness of space tells me that God has interests outside of earth, that he has his own relationship with the rest of the cosmos that we may or may not ever understand. I am reminded of the end of the book of Job, from chapter 38 onwards, when God speaks and reminds those assembled that he is in control of many things that humans do not comprehend, including the stars themselves.

For me, a black hole is like the creature that God describes called Leviathan – something mighty and powerful and beyond humanity's current ability to control or harness, and yet still a creation of God. And while I don't know God's reasons for creating it (and perhaps I never will), I am forever amazed and humbled that I have been given the ability to learn about it and study it from a distance. And perhaps one day, my understanding of it will be enough that I will learn something new about God as well.

One night, if the sky is clear and the moon is out, wrap up warm and go and look up at it. Keep looking until your brain realises that you're not just looking up – you're looking out, out into a universe more vast and more intricate than we're capable of imagining. Suddenly, your perspective shifts, and just for a moment you get a tiny sense of just how big everything is. I think that divine revelation must be a bit like that – getting to catch a glimpse of how God sees the universe. And, in a sense, that's exactly what I work towards in science as well.

9

Transformations and reactions

Marie Beale is a Messy Church leader in Bebington on the Wirral, and is also an Early Years teacher in Liverpool, where she gets lots of opportunities to be messy and help children to create. She studied natural sciences at university and has always been interested in the links between science and faith (and is rather fond of explosions).

Introduction

The dictionary says that a transformation is a 'marked change in form, nature, or appearance'. When you start to look carefully, you can see transformations all around you in the real world: adding baking powder to make a cake rise, whisking an egg to make meringue, spraying bleach on the stains on our kitchen worktops and many more. The change or metamorphosis of a caterpillar to a butterfly is amazing to watch.

The Bible also talks about transformation. Many Old Testament characters are seen being gradually or suddenly transformed: Abraham, Jacob, Joseph, among others. The story of the people of God can be read as a nation being transformed to become 'a light to the Gentiles'. Esther was transformed both in appearance and in her sense of purpose. Healing stories run through the Bible as God transforms people's health, mental, physical and spiritual. Jesus was 'transfigured' on the mountain. At Pentecost, the disciples are transformed from a terrified group of people to a fearless team of evangelists. The epistles continually urge their readers to become more holy in their thoughts, words and actions. Romans 12:2 says, 'Be transformed by the renewing of your mind.' The word Paul uses here is the word we use for that metamorphosis of a butterfly: total and complete change through the Holy Spirit. Perhaps the most amazing transformation of all history, I think, is from death to life through the resurrection of our Lord Jesus, making possible the miraculous transformation of ourselves on the other side of death.

Cornflour gloop

Ratings

MESS ♀♀♀♀♀   DANGER ♀♀♀♀♀   DIFFICULTY ♀♀♀♀♀

Theme

Crossing the Red Sea; walking on water; persons of the Holy Spirit; doubting/ standing firm

Equipment needed

A large flat plastic basin or tray; cornflour and water (or custard); spoons; aprons; bowl of water or sink to wash hands; towels

Before you begin

This is a classic activity for younger children but people of all ages love it. It is very messy but it will hoover up when dry and wash out of clothes. To keep mess to a minimum, put a towel under the table where you are experimenting, and make sure your bowls of water or sink are close by. You are exploring a 'non-Newtonian' substance, transforming from solid to liquid.

Experimental method

Start by adding 4–6 tablespoons of cornflour to the basin and gradually add water to make a thick liquid. Explore and play with the cornflour. Pick some up and let it flow through your fingers. Is it a solid or a liquid? What happens if you tap or punch the cornflour? (See photos online.)

If you have a small paddling pool and enough cornflour you should be able to run across the gloop (outside!). Alternatively, you could make up smaller pots of gloop for everyone to have their own.

Big thinking

Cornflour does not dissolve in water; it makes a suspension called a non-Newtonian fluid. Sometimes it seems to be like a solid (when we add force the particles jam together) and sometimes like a liquid (when the particles slip over each other and it flows through our fingers). When force is removed, water lubricates the particles and it becomes runny again.

Big questions

What happens to us when we are under pressure? How do we change? Have you ever felt stressed and unable to do something?

Jesus helps us when we are stressed: 'Come to me, all you who are weary and burdened, and I will give you rest' (Matthew 11:28). How can you come to Christ?

Sometimes we aren't sure and we waver, changing our minds. James 1:6 says, 'But when you ask, you must believe and not doubt, because the one who doubts is like a wave of the sea, blown and tossed by the wind.' How can we stand solid like a rock?

Mentos geyser

Ratings

MESS   DANGER   DIFFICULTY ...

Theme

Joy of the Holy Spirit; being witnesses of our faith; speaking gently (Proverbs)

Equipment needed

Packet of Mentos (mint sweets); two-litre bottle of fizzy lemonade or cola (with opening big enough for a Mento to fit in); plastic tray and mat; sheet of paper; towels

Before you begin

Make sure you test how many Mentos are needed to make your bottle explode.

Here you are producing a dramatic explosion as the Mentos transform the carbon dioxide to bubbles. People get very excited with this experiment – you are most likely to do it as a demonstration with people helping to put the Mentos in (although you could also give everyone their own smaller bottle to experiment with). There is potential to get covered in fizzy pop. Don't let people look down over the bottle, and if you get some in your eyes just rinse with warm water.

Experimental method

Ideally do this activity outside.

Open the bottle of fizzy drink (do not shake it first!) and stand it in the tray. Roll up a piece of paper to make a tube. Put the tube into the top of the bottle and pour in several sweets (different types of fizzy drink need different numbers of Mentos). Stand back quickly and watch what happens.

You could compare what happens if you put a Mento in a bottle of tap water. (Nothing.)

Big thinking

The drink is made fizzy by bubbles of invisible carbon dioxide which are added under pressure at the factory. When you open the bottle, bubbles form slowly. The surface of the Mentos is rough and has lots of tiny air pockets. When added to the drink the air allows large bubbles of carbon dioxide to form at the bottom of the bottle, pushing all the liquid up and out of the neck of the bottle. This process is called nucleation. A substance called gum arabic in the Mentos also reduces the surface tension of the drink, helping to form more bubbles.

Big questions

Who do you know who is bubbling over with faith, joy, hope, love and other character traits that God grows in us? What makes you overflow with excitement about your faith? How does our faith show God's energy and sparkle? God wants us to have new life in him, and the Bible says we are being raised from death to life. If you don't feel as if you're bubbling over with faith, can you think of anything you've heard or read about in church that might take you into that extra dimension and be the Mento to your cola?

Or perhaps more negatively, have you ever said something in a way that made someone else 'erupt'? The Bible tells us to be gentle with our words. Proverbs 15:1 says, 'A gentle answer turns away wrath, but a harsh word stirs up anger.'

Bicarbonate fizz

Ratings

MESS   DANGER   DIFFICULTY

Theme

Holy Spirit; anger (James 3)

Equipment needed

Water bottles; bicarbonate of soda; vinegar; paper funnels; balloons; food colouring; a plastic tray or baking tray

Before you begin

This can be a simple activity or a more complex one depending on what ages you want to include. We are watching what happens when we mix bicarbonate of soda (alkaline) and vinegar (acid) reacting to make carbon dioxide. Do supervise to make sure vinegar does not get squirted at others and young children do not eat the ingredients!

Experimental method

Pour vinegar into a small 250 ml water bottle about half full. Add two teaspoons of bicarbonate into a balloon using a funnel (you can make one with a paper cone). Stretch the mouth of the balloon over the mouth of the bottle, being careful not to let the bicarbonate fall into the bottle.

Lift the balloon and bottle completely upright so that the bicarbonate of soda in the balloon pours into the vinegar. Try different quantities of bicarbonate and vinegar. What happens?

And/or (younger children love this): have trays of a thin layer of bicarbonate and small shot glasses of vinegar mixed with food colouring. Drop the vinegar into the bicarbonate and watch how it fizzes.

Big thinking

The bicarbonate of soda and vinegar react with each other and make carbon dioxide (carbon dioxide gas). That makes the fizz you see in the trays. As the gas in the balloon can't escape, it blows up the balloon; the more bicarbonate and vinegar you combine, the more gas is made and the more the balloon blows up.

Big questions

The gas that fills the balloon is invisible but transformative: it changes the shape of the balloon. What visible and invisible 'ingredients' try to make your life change in some way? Are they life-giving or destructive?

What makes you 'blow up'? Why? It is easy to get angry or annoyed and we sometimes need self-control to stop our anger growing to the point where we say something we later wish we hadn't. According to James 3:2–8, our words can easily get out of control and fizz up. How can we stop? What would Jesus do?

Cleaning pennies

Ratings

MESS DANGER DIFFICULTY

Theme

Create in me a clean heart; forgiveness; the lost coin

Equipment needed

Dirty pennies; white vinegar; table salt; shallow plastic bowls; bowl of water; cloths/kitchen roll; disposable gloves (optional)

Before you begin

People find transforming a dull penny to its original sparkle by reacting copper oxide with vinegar and salt thrilling. For those with sensitive skin prone to eczema, disposable gloves can be worn.

Experimental method

Put your dirty pennies in the bowl and cover with salt. Pour over a little white vinegar and watch it fizz. Rub the salt and vinegar mix over both sides of the pennies.

Take the pennies out and wash off the mix in clean water. Buff to a shine.

Big thinking

Your pennies get dirty because they are made of copper which reacts with oxygen in the air to form copper oxide. When you put your pennies in a vinegar and salt mix, they react together, as vinegar is an acid and removes the copper oxide. (See photos online.)

You could try out other acids (such as lemon juice/orange juice) to see if they work as well.

Ask people what they think would happen if they don't rinse the pennies. Have some pennies you haven't rinsed and left to dry to show. They will be covered in a blue chemical called malachite.

Big questions

What things dull your sparkle? How can you get it back?

We need God to renew us and make us clean. The Bible says that when we are not with God we are like a lost coin (Luke 15:8–10). Do you want to be made clean?

Making ice cream

Ratings

MESS   DANGER   DIFFICULTY

Theme

Sermon on the Mount (salt and light); Romans 8:28

Equipment needed

Milk; cream (whipping or double); caster sugar; vanilla extract; salt; measuring jug; a large bag of ice (keep frozen until used); a small Ziploc bag and larger/1-litre Ziploc bag; stick or scientific thermometer; gloves or a tea towel; towels; bowls, cups, spoons or cones to serve your ice cream treat

Before you begin

This is one of my favourite activities, making ice cream by using salt and ice to cool and freeze the ingredients. It takes a little patience, and you may need gloves to stop hands getting too cold, especially with younger children.

Experimental method

Add 100 ml milk, 100 ml whipping or double cream, 50 g caster sugar and a few drops of vanilla extract to the small Ziploc bag and seal tightly. Add the ice and salt to the second bag and put the ingredient bag inside. Measure the temperature.

Hold the large bag at the top and move from side to side, using gloves or a tea towel to protect your hands, and towels for the floor/table. Be careful not to tear the bags with the ice. Continue this for 10–15 minutes or until the contents of the small bag have become thicker.

Open the large bag and use the thermometer to measure and record the temperature of the ice and salt mixture. This should be much colder than it was to begin with.

You could do this experiment twice (once with salt and once without) if you would like a comparison.

Big thinking

Things freeze when they reach their freezing point. Salt lowers water's freezing point and the low temperature is cold enough to change the cream from liquid to solid.

Big questions

What did you expect to happen with the mixture you had? Were you surprised? Has God ever surprised you?

What difference did the salt make to the experiment? Without salt the mixture would not have been cold enough to freeze. How can you be salt in your world to help other people know more about Jesus?

What are chips like without salt, or ice cream without sugar? Salt is a picture of the goodness of God in the world.

Elephant's toothpaste

Ratings

MESS   DANGER **DEMO ONLY** DIFFICULTY

Theme

Gifts and talents; Holy Spirit; God's love; Matthew 13 (God's kingdom)

Equipment needed

A large empty plastic lemonade bottle; washing-up bowl or builder's tray; hydrogen peroxide (ideally 6 per cent); packets of active yeast; washing-up liquid; food colouring (optional); warm water; safety glasses

Before you begin

This science experiment is spectacular, but uses chemicals which are potentially harmful, so we recommend doing it as a demonstration rather than a hands-on activity. Get a white coat and some safety glasses on and make it exciting! The chemicals can be bought from chemists or online.

Experimental method

Add a packet of yeast to a few tablespoons of warm water and leave it for a few minutes to froth up. Meanwhile, place the bottle in a washing-up bowl or builder's tray. Pour 5 cm of hydrogen peroxide (6 per cent) into the bottle and then squeeze in a good squirt of washing-up liquid.

Ask what people think will happen when you add the yeast. Pour in three tablespoons of the yeast solution. (See photos online.)

Big thinking

The chemical formula for hydrogen peroxide is H_2O_2. This is quite like the formula for water, which is H_2O, except that hydrogen peroxide has an extra oxygen 'O'. Hydrogen peroxide is not a very stable compound and decomposes to water and oxygen, but normally very slowly. In this reaction, yeast acts as a catalyst and speeds up the decomposition, making the reaction go much more quickly. If you add a little washing-up liquid and food colouring, you get coloured foam!

Big questions

What is your gift? How does God want you to use this gift? What is going to be the catalyst that makes you start using it?

Have you ever wished you had so much love that it would just pour over into other people's lives? How can this happen? How can we share that love with others?

Jesus used yeast in Matthew 13:33 to explain how God's kingdom appears to be small but can create something to change lives. How can we be catalysts to help ourselves and others change to be more like Jesus (Hebrews 10:24–25)?

Wind-up racer

Ratings

MESS  DANGER DIFFICULTY

Theme

God's energy – Isaiah 40:28–31, rising on eagles' wings; Philippians 4:13, 'I can do all this through him who gives me strength'

Equipment needed

Spool/cotton reel; skewer or crochet hook; sticky tape; washer or slice of candle with wick removed (no bigger than the diameter of the cotton reel); pencil; rubber band (full sized, but just long enough to fit through your spool)

Before you begin

I used to make these wind-up racers as a child, and was always excited to find my mum had finished a reel of thread. You can buy wooden or plastic spools online; I prefer the wooden but the plastic will still work well.

Experimental method

Feed the rubber band through the cotton reel using a skewer (or a crochet hook). Use a matchstick or break off some of your skewer and put on one end so that it doesn't poke out. Tape it on. (See diagrams online.)

Thread the rubber band at the other end through the washer and put the pencil through the loop in the band. Move the pencil round and round to 'wind up your tank'.

Put it on a flat surface and watch it go. Adjust the length of your band or pencil and see what happens.

Big thinking

When you use your energy to wind up your elastic band with the pencil, you create potential energy in the elastic band. Potential energy is energy that has the ability to do work in the future, but is not currently performing any work. The more you wind up, the more potential energy you make. When you put your racer down, the elastic band unwinds and converts the potential energy into kinetic or moving energy as the spool rolls across the surface.

Big questions

'That energy is *God's* energy, an energy deep within you, God himself willing and working at what will give him the most pleasure' (Philippians 2:13, THE MESSAGE).

Another translation of the same passage says, 'For it is God who works in you to will and to act in order to fulfill his good purpose.'

God creates potential energy in us. How can you use that energy? When do you feel you are running out of energy? What keeps you going? What promises does God make about energy? Read Colossians 1:11, 29.

Sun prints

Ratings

MESS   DANGER   DIFFICULTY

Theme

'I am the light of the world'; let your light shine; the glory of God (Revelation 21)

Equipment needed

Photo-sensitive (sun print) paper; acrylic sheets (e.g. Ikea frame inners); cardboard; a tub full of water; fun and interesting objects to print

Experimental method

Arrange your objects on a piece of photo-sensitive paper away from sunlight (not near a window). Place a clear acrylic sheet on to your paper, take it outside and lay it in direct sunlight for two to five minutes.

The areas of the paper exposed to the sun will fade. When you see most of the colour disappear from the paper, your print has been fully exposed. If it is cloudy this may take up to 15 minutes.

Take all the items off and rinse your print in water for a couple of minutes to stop the reaction.

Watch what happens. Lay your print flat on a paper towel and allow it to dry.

Big thinking

The paper is coated with special light-sensitive chemicals, and then dried and stored in a light-proof bag. The items you place on to it block the light and the sun/light causes the paper around the objects to change colour. Water stops the reaction and fixes the image.

Big questions

Even on a cloudy day, the sun can transform the paper and make a sharp image. God sees the details of our lives in sharp focus, too. How does that make you feel?

Talk about Ephesians 5:13–14: 'But everything exposed by the light becomes visible – and everything that is illuminated becomes a light. This is why it is said: "Wake up, sleeper, rise from the dead, and Christ will shine on you."'

When light shines in darkness it transforms the darkness. Why do you think Jesus tells us to be like lights? How can we do this?

Types of invisible ink

Ratings

MESS   DANGER   DIFFICULTY

Theme

Secrets; parables

Equipment needed

Method 1: Baking soda; paper; bowl; brushes and cotton buds; balsamic vinegar; tablecloth; a hairdryer (optional)

Method 2: Milk; bowl; paper; brushes and cotton buds; an iron

Before you begin

Most of us have written secret messages sometime. Here we look at two types of secret messages and the science behind them.

Experimental method

Method 1

Mix about four tablespoons of baking soda and four tablespoons of water together. Write a secret message with a cotton bud or a brush dipped in the solution. Let the paper dry (use a hairdryer on low heat if you want it done sooner).

To read the secret message, paint over it gently and thinly with balsamic vinegar. Protect the table you are working on with a tablecloth, as the vinegar can stain.

Method 2

Pour some milk into a bowl and write a message with it on a piece of paper with a cotton bud or brush. Let your message dry completely.

This time, when you want to read your message, just heat the paper. Ask an adult to iron over it. Your message will appear.

Big thinking

In Method 1, the vinegar has an acid that reacts with the baking soda. So a different colour appears and shows the writing.

In Method 2, milk contains water and fat. When it dries, the water evaporates, leaving the fat on the paper. When you heat the paper, the fat turns brown and your invisible message appears.

Big questions

Do you have any secrets which weigh on your mind? God knows them. Can you share them with him openly?

Do you sometimes wish God would be more obvious? Why do you think it feels as if he's hiding from us sometimes? How would you like him to show himself?

Read Luke 8:17 and 12:2–3. Sometimes Jesus' words were hard to understand, and only made sense after he was crucified and rose again. Your secret message meant nothing until it could be seen. What clues do we see in our world today to show God at work?

Slime

Ratings

MESS   DANGER 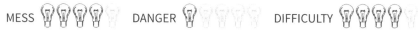   DIFFICULTY

Theme

Sin; being shaped by God

Equipment needed

Aldi Almat bio gel; PVA glue; food colouring (optional); measuring jug; teaspoon; a large bowl; washing-up bowls; disposable vinyl gloves (avoid latex if possible)

Before you begin

Slime is a wonderful sensory material all ages enjoy playing with. You will find a lot of US recipes that contain materials which are difficult to source in the UK. This version uses Aldi green Almat bio gel and PVA glue only.

Experimental method

Use 100 ml of glue and add a teaspoon of the bio gel. Mix it up and add more gel, little by little until you can knead the slime/putty without it sticking to your fingers. (See photos online.) Roll out and knead. If it is too sticky, add more gel a drop at a time until it is firm enough to play with. Add food colouring if you wish.

Big thinking

PVA glue is polyvinyl acetate, a liquid polymer. There is borax in the Almat bio gel. This links the PVA molecules to each other, creating one large, flexible polymer. This kind of slime will get stiffer and more like putty the more you play with it.

Big questions

When you hold the slime it 'flows' and covers everything around. That is like sin; sinful things can look like fun but soon mess up lots of areas of our lives. What has Jesus done about the things that mess us up? When we become Christians, God takes us and starts to mould and shape us like you have been moulding the slime. Read Isaiah 64:8. How have you been moulded?

Perspective

Nick Higgs is a marine biologist and Deputy Director of the Marine Institute, Plymouth University.

The next time that you are at the beach or in the woods, stop and find the tiniest animal that you can see. Then watch it for a bit, going about its business. It has its own little life. All over the world, even in the deepest depths of the ocean, there are millions and millions of creatures doing their own thing, playing their part in the world. What are they all doing? Why do they do what they do? When I was little, these were the kind of questions I thought about and this curiosity is probably the reason that I became a scientist.

As a marine biologist, these are still the kinds of questions that I think about in my job. I try to understand what animals do in the environment and how their actions keep the whole ecosystem working. Most of my work looks at how organisms get recycled in the oceans when they die. One of the weirdest animals I study are bone-eating worms called *Osedax* (say Oz-ee-dax) that live on the skeletons of dead whales at the bottom of the ocean. They turn the bones into food and eventually become food for other animals themselves, in a complicated food web. What a strange way to make a living! Nevertheless, they are playing their part in keeping life going.

We can so easily think that the whole world is just about us humans, but we are just one part of a complicated and wonderful system of life. Although we are particularly special to God, I think he cares about all of his creation. Psalm 104 describes how God looks after all the plants and animals that live on earth, providing them with the food they need. Jesus reminds us that 'not a single sparrow can fall to the ground without your Father [God] knowing it' (Matthew 10:29, NLT). If God cares so much about his creation, I think we should too. That is partly why I feel God wants me to be a scientist.

Another reason that I enjoy science is because it teaches me about God. Paul wrote that 'through everything God made, [we] can clearly see his invisible qualities – his eternal power and divine nature' (Romans 1:20, NLT). Both the Bible and the world around us came from God and each has something to teach us about him. Some think that they come up with conflicting answers, but that is impossible if they both come from God. If someone thinks there is a conflict between the Bible and science, they are interpreting one of them incorrectly. It is important to study both together, and that is exactly what I do as a scientist.

When I was about seven years old, I was fascinated by the idea that even the tiniest ants that crawled on my finger each had a brain. How can you fit all of that into a tiny ant? Was it like my brain and does it do the same things? These are not new questions. One of the writers of the Proverbs marvels at the way ants are so small but 'unusually wise' (30:24, NLT). These are exactly the kinds of questions that science can and has answered. It might seem trivial to think about the mind of an ant, but some of the great insights into the evolution of cooperative behaviour have come from studying ants. Understanding ants has helped us understand why we might care about other people.

The naturalist John Muir said, 'When we try to pick out anything by itself, we find it hitched to everything else in the universe.' This is what I find so exciting about science. Every new discovery leads you on to something else because it is all connected. Never stop asking questions because there is a lot more to learn, both about the world around us and about God. Ultimately that connection is God, who holds all creation together.

10

Time and measurement

Revd Dr **David Gregory** is Senior Minister of Croxley Green Baptist Church and has a background in physics, astronomy, meteorology and climate. He is the 2017–18 Vice-President of the Baptist Union.

Introduction

Science involves watching how things move, change and interact with each other. An important part of this is taking accurate measurements of length, heat, weight and time.

The Bible also talks about measurement. In the stories of creation at the start of the Bible, God makes the sun and the moon to 'mark the seasons, days and years' (Genesis 1:14, NLT). The rainbow after the flood was a sign that the seasons would continue. And there are places where people are told to measure quantities accurately, for example in Leviticus 19:36: 'Use honest scales and honest weights.' Of course, this was about trading with people fairly, but accurate measurements and honesty are just as important in science as we try to understand how the world works. God is described as God of eternity, outside time and Lord of past, present and future 'who was and is and is to come', which is a dimension that is hard for many of us to wrap our minds around.

A pendulum clock

Ratings

MESS 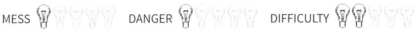 DANGER DIFFICULTY

Theme

Measuring time and seasons

Equipment needed

A table with a top 75–100 cm off the floor; a pencil or wooden rod (it needs to be long enough to extend 5 cm beyond the end of the table); string; several medium-sized metal nuts; a paper clip; sticky tape; stopwatch or timer; paper; pencil

Before you begin

In this experiment we are going to make a pendulum. Hold a piece of string with a metal nut attached to the bottom between your fingers. Move the nut to one side and allow it to swing to and fro. If you know how long it takes to swing back to where it started (this is called its period), then you can use it to measure how time passes by counting the swings.

Explain that you are going to investigate what makes the period of the swing take different times. You might want people to suggest what might make the time of the period change – what about the weight on the end; the area of the weight; the length of the string?

Experimental method

Fix the pencil or wooden rod on to the table so it overlaps by 4–5 cm. Cut a piece of string 15 cm shorter than the height of the table and tie it to the pencil or wooden rod. Make a small hook from the paper clip so you can hang the metal nuts on it. Attach the hook to the bottom of the string. Place a nut on to the string.

Get your timer ready. Set the pendulum swinging and count how many swings – from where it starts to when it gets back there again – it goes through in one minute. If you divide 60 – the number of seconds in a minute – by the number of swings, you will calculate the period of the pendulum. You might want to do this several times to see how good you are at measuring. Do you get the same answers all the time?

Now add two more nuts on to the hook. Repeat your measurements as above. What happens to the period of the pendulum?

Finally, reduce the length of the string of the pendulum by between a third and a half – the simplest way to do this is to tie the hook on higher up. Now what happens to the period of the swing?

Big thinking

The period of a pendulum only depends upon its length and not on the size of the weight at its end. So if you know the length of the pendulum, you can calculate its period and so have a way of keeping the time. This is how old-fashioned 'grandfather' and 'grandmother' clocks worked – perhaps you have seen one in a museum or even at home.

But the period also depends upon the strength of gravity. So if you went to a planet that had less gravity than the earth, the period would get longer. And if the planet had stronger gravity than the earth, it would get shorter.

Big questions

Talk about how the creation story in the Bible speaks about the regular motions of the sun and moon marking the times and seasons through the year.

As people watch the pendulum go back and forth, ask them to think about what their favourite time of year is and give thanks to God.

Barton's pendulum

Ratings

MESS   DANGER    DIFFICULTY

Theme

Keeping in step with God

Equipment needed

Two stepladders (or two hooks on opposite walls); string; medium and small metal nets; small circular pieces of colourful paper, 4 cm across; sticky tape

Before you begin

Set up the main equipment by tying a long piece of string between the two stepladders or hooks on either side of the room. (See photo online.)

Prepare two pieces of string about 1 m long – they need to be shorter than the height off the floor of the string stretched across the room. Take one of the pieces of string and attach several of the large nuts to the bottom to make a pendulum. You may need to stick the nuts together to do this. Attach the pendulum near to one end of the string stretched out across the room. This is the driver pendulum.

Take the other piece of string and attach one of the medium-sized nuts to it. Attach this to the middle of the string stretched out across the room. You will need to ensure that, once tied on, it is the same length as the 'driver pendulum'.

Take a circular piece of paper, cut a slit from the edge to the centre and slide over the string of each pendulum. Slide the two sides of the cut over each other to make a small cone, sticking this in place. Slide it down over the string to cover the nuts at the bottom of the pendulum. Do this for both of the pendulums.

Experimental method

Cut more pieces of string, ensuring that they are shorter than the length of the 'driver' pendulum. Attach a small nut to each of the strings, and also a small cone using the coloured piece of paper as described above. It is best to use different colours from those of the two longest pendulums.

Tie the shorter pendulums on the string stretched across the room around the long pendulum in the centre. Make sure that the string stretched across the room is still tight when you do this. (See photo online.)

If you have made 'A pendulum clock' (see p. 233), ask what is important in determining how fast a pendulum will swing (the length). Explain that you are going to start the 'driver' (big) pendulum going. This will twist the string to which all the other pendulums are attached. Ask: what do you think will happen? Will they start to move? Which will move fastest? Which will move the most?

You may need to keep the driver pendulum going from time to time. After a while, all the pendulums should begin to move a little. But the one that is the same length as the driver pendulum will move the most. But does it match the driver pendulum exactly? (Note: when the driver pendulum is at the far end of its swing, the other pendulum of the same length should be going through its mid-point – a quarter of a swing behind.) Ask: does the way the pendulums move – or don't move – surprise people?

Big thinking

The length of the swing of the pendulum depends upon its length. The 'driver' pendulum twists the string back and forth with the same period as it takes to swing. This moves energy from the 'driver' pendulum to the other pendulums, causing them to move. But only the other pendulum the same length is happy to swing at this rate. Because they are shorter, the other pendulums want to move at a faster rate. They cannot pick up as much energy, so only move a little. The pendulums the same length swinging together is an example of resonance.

What would happen if the 'driver' pendulum was the same length as one of the shorter pendulums? You might want to try it and see what happens.

Big questions

As people watch the pendulums move, ask them to think about the following questions:
- How are you following God's leading?
- What or whom are you following?
- What stops you keeping in step with God?

Sand timers

Ratings

MESS   DANGER   DIFFICULTY

Theme

Waiting; patience

Equipment needed

Two 250 ml plastic bottles with pull-up sports caps (best if they have several little holes in the cap rather than a large hole); silver sand; strong sticky tape e.g. gaffa tape; a piece of A4 paper; plastic bowl; timer

Before you begin

Ask if people know how you measure time; clocks, watches, computers and phones might be mentioned. How might people have measured time before modern inventions? This time they might mention water and sand timers or the motions of the sun and moon.

Experimental method

Connect the two sports caps together so that the two bottles can be joined together later. Ensure that both caps are fully open before you fix with the strong tape. (Note: If they only have a single large hole, you will need to place something between them to restrict the width of the opening, such as a small piece of card with several holes in it large enough for the sand to flow through. You may need to experiment with this before connecting the caps to ensure the sand flows through smoothly.)

Roll up the paper to make a cone, leaving a small opening in the bottom. Using the cone, spoon sand into one of the bottles. You will need to estimate how much sand you need for the time to measure one minute.

Screw the caps on to the bottle with the sand in and turn it over so the sand flows into the bowl. Using the timer, see how much sand flows out in a minute. Once a minute is up, stop the sand flowing out of the bottle.

If, after one minute, there is still sand in the bottle, discard this. If the sand flowed out in less than a minute, add more sand into the bowl. Return the sand to the bottle and repeat so that you have enough sand to flow from the bottle in one minute. Screw the second bottle on to its cap to complete the timer. (See photo online.)

Turn it over a few times to check how long it takes for the sand to go from one bottle to the other. Is it the same in each direction? Why do you think this might be or not be?

Big thinking

The sand flows from one side of the timer to the other as it is pulled down by gravity. You could try materials other than sand – like flour or water or small seeds. Do you think you would need more or less of each of these to measure the same amount of time? Why would that be? What else might determine the amount of sand or other material that you might need?

There are lots of factors that might change the time the sand or other material takes to flow through: for example, how slippery it is (this is determined by how much the small particles of the material rub against each other, called friction); how big the hole is between the two halves of the timer.

If you have done the pendulum experiment, ask people if the sand timer is a better way of measuring time. In fact, because of all the different factors that can affect the flow of the sand, measuring time using a pendulum is more accurate as it only depends upon the length of the string.

Big questions

Ask people to watch the sand flowing from one bottle to the other.

While they do so, invite them to think about:
- Something they are waiting for; how do they feel about waiting?
- What they need patience for; ask God to help them when it is hard
- How patient God is: how is he patient with us? What might that mean for how we need to grow? (See Galatians 5:22, NRSV: 'the fruit of the spirit is… patience'.)

A slice of Pi

Ratings

MESS 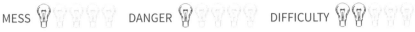 DANGER DIFFICULTY

Theme

The constancy of God and God's love

Equipment needed

Different-sized circular objects (cups, saucers, plates of different sizes, etc.); string; pen; ruler; calculator; sticky tape

Before you begin

Ask your participants what is the same and what is different about the objects. (All circles; all different sizes.) You are going to show that circles are always the same despite appearing to be different.

Experimental method

Place each circular object flat on a table. Take the string and fix one end to the edge of the object using a small piece of sticky tape. Place the string around the circular edge of the object so that it stretches around to the beginning – mark this with the pen on the string. Measure the length of the string that fits around the circular edge of the object: this is called the circumference of the circle.

Take a ruler and measure the width across the circle, making sure you measure from edge to edge through the centre of the circle. If it is too big for the ruler, measure it using the string. This is called the diameter of the circle.

Using the calculator, divide the length of the circumference by the length of the diameter. Make a note of this number along with the circumference and diameter on a piece of paper.

Repeat for different-sized circular objects.

Big thinking

What do you notice about how the number you have calculated from the circumference and diameter changes with the size of the circle? It should be roughly the same. Why do you think it might be different between different-sized circles? Do they follow different rules of how their diameter and circumference are related? Or how could you make your measurements more accurate? If you did the experiment again, do you get the same answer?

In fact, if you have measured it very accurately, it should be the same for every circle. It is a very special number called 'Pi': 3.14125927. But the number does not stop there – it goes on for ever and ever, and the numbers never, ever repeat. You could look up on the internet how big it can get!

You can find the number Pi in the Bible. In 1 Kings 7:23–24, a circular basin is described which is 'ten cubits' across and 'thirty cubits' around. How accurate is their value of Pi?

Big questions

Talk about how, like Pi, God is infinite – going on for ever and ever! And God is constant and never changing in a world which is always changing. While we are all different, his love for us is always the same.

Measuring direction: a water compass

Ratings

MESS 💡 💡 💡 💡 💡   DANGER 💡 💡 💡 💡 💡   DIFFICULTY 💡 💡 💡 💡 💡

Theme

Who are you following?

Equipment needed

Two bar magnets; a plastic bowl; a paper clip; wire cutters; scissors; foil container from a night light; a small coloured triangular-shaped piece of paper; a compass; water

Before you begin

Show people the bar magnets. Explain that some metals have a special property called a magnetic field. It spreads from one end of the bar of metal – or pole – to the other. Each magnet has a north pole and a south pole. You cannot see it, but you can see what it does.

Bring the north poles of the magnets together – what do they do? (They should push each other away.) Bring the north and south poles together – what do they do? (They should attract each other and stick together.)

The earth is also like a huge magnet and you can use a small magnet to help you find which direction is north. This is how people used to navigate before satnavs.

Experimental method

Take the bowl and fill it half full with water. Straighten the paper clip and cut it so that it is just longer than the small night light foil tray. Hold the paper clip out between your thumb and first finger. Now take one of the magnets and run the north pole of the magnet along the length of the paper clip. Repeat this between 10 and 20 times, always with the north pole running along the length of the paper clip. This will magnetise the paper clip.

Cut two small slits on opposite sides of the foil tray and secure the paper clip across it. Now float the tray and paper clip in the water and spin it around a little. What direction does it come to rest pointing in? Compare this to the direction of north using the compass. If they agree, attach the small triangular piece of paper to the end of the paper clip pointing north. If not, then try magnetising the paper clip again. (See photo online.)

Big thinking

Any material is made up of particles called atoms – and these are made up of even smaller particles. In the centre of the atom there are particles called protons and neutrons and, orbiting around them (a bit like planets orbit the sun), are even smaller particles called electrons. These are also spinning around, just like the earth does on its axis. They have a negative electric charge and each has a small magnetic field. Usually they all spin in different directions, but by running the magnet over the paper clip, the electrons start to spin in the same direction, all their magnetic fields add together and the paper clip becomes magnetic. The south pole of the magnetic paper clip is then attracted to the north pole of the earth.

The earth is a huge magnet because at its centre is a large ball of molten iron which spins around, generating a magnetic field. The earth's magnetic field is very important for life. It goes a long way out into space and protects the earth from harmful radiation from the sun which would hurt life.

Big questions

Spin the compass around. Think of Jesus' words to some fishermen – 'Follow me.' How are you following Jesus? How have you not been following Jesus? What would Jesus want you to be like at school, at home, at work?

Think about how the earth's magnetic field protects life on earth. Think or talk about who or what might protect you from danger. How does God protect us from being hurt? How might following God's way protect us?

Measuring temperature:
a water thermometer

Ratings

MESS 💡 💡 💡 💡   DANGER 💡 💡 💡 💡   DIFFICULTY 💡 💡 💡 💡

Theme

Living for God; climate change

Equipment needed

500 ml empty water bottle; straw (transparent or light coloured); blu-tack; scissors; an A4 piece of paper; glass flat-bottomed bowl; hot and cold water; blue food colouring

Before you begin

You might ask what things around the home help to measure how hot something is. People might suggest a thermostat linked to the central heating system, or a thermometer in the kitchen or in the fridge.

What is temperature measured in? Degrees centigrade – 0 degrees centigrade is the freezing point of water, while 100 degrees centigrade is the boiling point of water.

Explain that we are going to make a simple thermometer.

Experimental method

Quarter fill the water bottle with cold water from a tap. Add some blue food colouring. Use the scissors to make a hole in the bottle cap (or use a sports bottle which already has a hole) and slide the straw through. Fix the cap back on to the bottle and adjust the straw until it dips into the water by about 1 cm. Use the blu-tack to seal around the straw to make it airtight.

Note the level of the water in the straw – it should be same as the level of the water in the bottle.

Place the bottle into the flat-bottomed bowl. Mix hot and cold water in equal measure and place the water in the bowl. The water level in the straw should rise. Mark the level on the bottle. (See photo online.)

Replace the water with hotter water. What happens to the level of water in the straw? It should start to rise further up the straw.

Be careful not to squeeze the bottles otherwise it will get messy!

Big thinking

Ask people how they think the thermometer works. Explain that as the water in the bottle warms it expands, rising up the straw. The warmer the water is, the higher the water rises up the straw. The air in the top of the bottle will also expand as it warms, also helping to push the water up the straw.

If people are taking the water thermometer home, ask them to place it in different parts of the house – in a sunny window, in the fridge or on a radiator – and see what happens to the water.

What are the disadvantages of using water as the liquid inside the thermometer? What would happen at the freezing point of water (0 degrees centigrade) or the boiling point (100 degrees centigrade)? The water would freeze or boil away. This is why thermometers often use a metal called mercury, which is a liquid over a wider range of temperatures (-38 to 356 degrees centigrade).

Big questions

Read Revelation 3:15: 'I know your deeds, that you are neither cold nor hot. I wish you were either one or the other!' Think about hot food you like. Do you enjoy it when it is lukewarm? Or a nice cold drink of water; is it as refreshing when it is lukewarm? Talk about whether our actions share God's love and life.

Think about people who are struggling with the effects of climate change – where it is getting too hot to live because the earth is warming, or places that are being flooded because ice is melting.

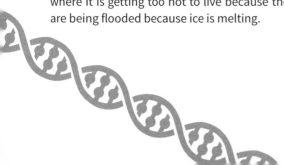

Weighing air

Ratings

MESS    DANGER   DIFFICULTY

Theme

God gives life

Equipment needed

Several items of different weights (such as a bag of sugar or sweets); coat hanger; bamboo BBQ skewer (with sharp end cut off); two balloons; string; blu-tack; kitchen scales (measuring parts of a gram); balloon pump (optional)

Before you begin

Invite people to feel the various items of different weights. Have them put them in order of how heavy they feel. You might want to check if they are right, using the kitchen scales. This part of the experiment works better if you put the items into unmarked boxes or bags (as opposed to their original packaging), so no one can cheat!

Ask if they think air has any weight.

Experimental method

Mark the mid-point of the skewer with a marker pen, and also 1 cm from each end. At the mid-point of the skewer, attach a piece of string. Do not tie the knot too tightly, to allow the skewer to slide through. Then attach the other end of the string to the coat hanger so the skewer hangs freely below. This is a simple balance that can be used to compare weights.

Attach the two uninflated balloons to either end of the skewer. Hang the coat hanger from a door frame or from a string stretched across the room. If the balloons are the same weight, the skewer should be level. If not, then adjust the position of the string at the centre of the skewer until the balloons are balanced.

Remove one of the balloons and inflate it. Reattach to the skewer and rehang the balance. How does it hang now? The end with the inflated balloon should be lower.

Take a small piece of blu-tack and add to the side of the balance with the uninflated balloon. Keep adding small amounts until the balance is level again.

Big thinking

When the balloons are uninflated they have the same weight, so the balance is level. But the inflated balloon has air in it so it is heavier, causing the balance to tip. The amount of blu-tack added to the other end of the balance is the same weight of the air in the balloon. You could measure this weight on kitchen scales, but they need to be very accurate and be able to measure parts of a gram.

Air does not seem to have any weight, but the atmosphere above our heads weighs 10,000 kg – the equivalent of 10,000 bags of sugar pushing down on us!

Another way we know air has weight is wind. When it is very strong, it can push objects and people around. If air did not have weight it would not be able to do this and we would not be able to feel it pushing us on a windy day.

Big questions

We probably don't notice air very much – we pass through it every day. There are times when we do not seem very important either to others. But the story of human creation in the Bible says we are alive because God has placed his 'breath' – his spirit – in us. Read Genesis 2:7: 'Then the Lord God formed a man from the dust of the ground and breathed into his nostrils the breath of life, and the man became a living being.'

Get people to breathe in and out several times, pausing between breaths to think about how special each one of us is to God, how he gives us life and how he shares his life with us.

Hard-boiled egg?

Ratings

MESS    DANGER   DIFFICULTY

Theme

Seeking truth

Equipment needed

Two eggs (one raw, one hard-boiled) of similar size and weight; permanent marker pens; flat-bottomed bowl; kitchen scales

Before you begin

Explain that in doing scientific experiments, making accurate observations is important to finding out the answer to questions we ask about what things are like or how something works. You are going to use different methods – without cracking the shells – to try and determine which of two eggs is raw, and which is hard-boiled. We are looking for any differences between the eggs that we can find.

Experimental method

Begin by marking the eggs 1 and 2 with the marker pen.

1   Weigh the eggs. Is one heavier than the other?
2   Put both eggs in water. Do they float or sink? Do you notice any difference in how they sit in the water?
3   While they are in the water, try and spin them. Do they behave differently?
4   Take them out of the water and place them on a smooth surface. Spin each of them and then stop them with your finger. How do they behave?

Based upon your observations, which egg is the hard-boiled one? Once you have made your choice, crack one on your head. You might want to have kitchen towel available just in case you make the wrong choice!

Big thinking

Whether hard-boiled or raw, the eggs should weigh about the same. They both should also sink in water, but while the hard-boiled egg lies on its side, the raw egg will lie more vertically. This is because the small amount of air inside the egg is free to move around and so goes to the top. Also, the hard-boiled egg will spin easily underwater, while the raw egg does not spin as well. On a smooth surface, both eggs will spin easily, but while the hard-boiled egg will stop when it is touched, the raw egg will continue to spin.

The difference in the behaviour of the eggs when they spin is that one is a solid, while the other is filled with a fluid. The hard-boiled egg spins at the same speed all the way through. When it is stopped, all parts of it stop at the same time. When the raw egg is stopped, only the shell is stopped – the inside fluid still spins, and this makes the shell start to spin again. This behaviour is the main way to determine if the egg is raw or hard-boiled.

Big questions

Read Luke 6:43–45: 'No good tree bears bad fruit, nor does a bad tree bear good fruit. Each tree is recognised by its own fruit. People do not pick figs from thorn-bushes, or grapes from briers. A good man brings good things out of the good stored up in his heart, and an evil man brings evil things out of the evil stored up in his heart. For the mouth speaks what the heart is full of.'

Talk about how we might know if people are trustworthy. We cannot look inside them, but we can look at how they behave and act towards others.

How fast are you?

Ratings

MESS   DANGER   DIFFICULTY

Theme

Amazing abilities God gives; God is slow to anger but quick to forgive

Equipment needed

A 30 cm ruler; a scientific calculator

Before you begin

Ask people how you could measure how fast they might be. They might mention timing people in a running race like the 100 m. But getting a good start in a race is important, and that depends on how fast your body can respond to the starting signal. And that depends on how quickly your brain can hear the starting signal and send a signal to your muscles to respond.

Experimental method

Get someone to hold the ruler in the air, holding it from the '30 cm' end. Place the '0 cm' end between the open thumb and first finger of a second volunteer. The person holding the ruler lets it drop without warning. The other person tries to stop it falling with their thumb and first finger. Read off the distance on the ruler where the thumb and first finger have grabbed the ruler.

You could mix this up by trying different methods. For example, get the catcher to close their eyes and respond to a countdown.

Big thinking

The distance the ruler falls before it is caught depends upon how fast you react to the starting signal. The faster your reaction time, the shorter the distance the ruler will fall. You can calculate your reaction time from the distance on the ruler.

Convert the distance from centimetres to metres by dividing by 100. Multiply the distance by 2 and divide by 10, which is approximately the acceleration due to gravity (measured in metres per second squared). This is how fast the gravity of the earth pulls things downwards. After falling for one second, an object has a speed of 10 metres per second; after falling for two seconds 20 metres per second, and so on. Use the scientific calculator to take the square root (the '√' key) to give you your reaction time. Or you can use the estimates in the table below.

Distance (cm)	Distance (m)	Reaction time
1	0.01	0.045
2	0.02	0.063
5	0.05	0.100
10	0.10	0.141
15	0.15	0.173
20	0.20	0.200
25	0.25	0.224
30	0.30	0.245

Who is the fastest? Does a person's age have any effect? Reaction times slow down as people get older. If the person dropping the ruler told you when they were going to let it go, was your reaction time faster?

Big questions

Read Psalm 139:13–14: 'For you created my inmost being; you knit me together in my mother's womb. I praise you because I am fearfully and wonderfully made.'

Talk about the amazing abilities that we have and the amazing way our bodies work together to do things.

Light speed

Ratings

MESS   DANGER   DIFFICULTY

Theme

God and light

Equipment needed

Bar of chocolate (it needs to be 20–30 cm long at least); ruler; plastic bowl or cup with flat bottom; glass plate; microwave oven

Before you begin

Light is all around us and travels at the fastest speed of anything in the universe – so fast that you cannot see light move across a room. But we can measure how fast it is moving using a microwave oven and a bar of chocolate!

Microwaves are a form of light that our eyes cannot see. But we come across them in everyday life. They are used to send signals between our mobile phone, and in kitchens to cook food. Microwaves cause water molecules in food to vibrate, which we can feel as the food gets hot.

Experimental method

Note: You will need to know the frequency of the microwave used in the microwave oven. This will be written somewhere on the oven, typically on the back or inside the door. Commonly the frequency is 2,450MHz – that is, 2,450,000,000 cycles of the wave every second.

Firstly, remove the rotating tray from the microwave. Place the plastic bowl or cup over the centre of the oven and place the heat-resistant glass plate on top. Place the bar of chocolate across the centre of the plate. It is best if the bar extends right across the plate – you may need to use parts of more than one bar to do this.

Microwave on full power for 20 seconds (the exact time will depend upon the power of the microwave). Parts of the bar will have melted – you may need to test it using a knife. Measure the distance between the melted parts (typically between 6 and 7 cm). (See photo online.) This is half the wave length of the microwaves – the distance between the start and end of one cycle of the wave.

Convert the wave length from centimetres to metres if necessary (divide by 100) and then multiply by the frequency of the microwaves. The resulting number is the speed of light in metres per second.

Once you have finished your experiment, you can eat the chocolate (once it has cooled).

Big thinking

Light travels at 299,792,458 metres per second – how close did your answers come? Why do you think they might be different? It could be that it was hard to measure the distance between the melted chocolate accurately as the heat from the part that is melted spreads along the bar. Try using a shorter time to microwave the bar of chocolate to see if you can get a better estimate of the wave length by melting a smaller part of the chocolate. This is what scientists call reducing experimental error to get more accurate measurements.

You might not be able to see light move across a room, but the distances of space are so vast that it takes eight minutes for light to travel from the sun to the earth, and over four years for light to travel to the nearest star. And light from the farthest galaxy seen so far has taken more than 13 billion years to travel to the earth – that is nearly three times longer than scientists estimate the age of the earth to be!

Big questions

Talk about how the Bible speaks about God using light. Do the facts you've explored about light here make you think about Jesus differently?

- 1 John 1:5: 'God is light' – The perfection of God
- John 8:12: 'I am the light of the world' – Jesus shows us God's perfect life
- Matthew 5:14: 'You are the light of the world' – When we follow Jesus, God shines his life through us
- How can you measure someone's love for you? Are there some things it's impossible to measure? What measure of love would you say is visible in the cross of Jesus?

Perspective

The Revd Canon Dr **Joanna Collicutt** is a clinical neuropsychologist with many years' experience of working with people living with conditions affecting the brain, including dementia, and is Advisor for Spiritual Care for Older People (SCOP) in the Oxford Diocese.

I was the sort of annoying little girl who wondered about stuff, asked awkward questions and looked smug when my teachers couldn't answer. I was once told that God made everything, so I asked who made God. 'God made himself!' snapped the teacher. I was at primary school when the first people went into space and I wondered why none of them had seen God; wasn't he supposed to live up there? I asked my teachers about this, too, but they just looked a bit shifty.

Later, as I learned more about science, I decided that we didn't really need the idea of God at all because we could explain the universe without him. I wasn't sure what to make of Jesus; I came to the conclusion that he was a good man but that the stories of his miracles and his resurrection had been made up by his followers and embellished with superstitious myths. By the age of ten, I was an atheist.

But a few years later something changed my mind. We had a visiting preacher at our church. He wasn't particularly inspiring but he said something that I have never forgotten: 'A person who thinks that science has proved that God doesn't exist is like a child who thinks that 13 x 13 doesn't exist because he only knows his times tables up to 12 x 12.' What that preacher couldn't have known is that I had made exactly this mistake a while back when being tested on my tables by my father. (In those days we learnt them by rote up to 12 x 12 = 144.) I was good at arithmetic and I knew it. Daddy couldn't trip me up and my smugness irritated him. So he thought outside the box and asked me to calculate 13 x 13. Without pausing to think I said, 'It doesn't exist!' and immediately realised how stupid I had been. Just because something is beyond our experience and knowledge, or even beyond our mental capacities, doesn't mean that it doesn't exist.

I was totally shocked. First I realised that I might have been wrong about science and God – some things may be beyond science. But much more importantly, I started to wonder about what God might be like. Could it be that there was a God who had known me all along as an inquisitive little girl and later as a budding mathematician, and who took the trouble to connect with me through my life story? Perhaps this is what people meant when they said that God 'spoke' – perhaps you didn't have to hear physical words; perhaps God communicated in subtle ways known only to you and him. Had God done this with me and, if so, why? Could it be that I was important to him? Could it be that God cared about me – even liked me, with all my irritating smugness?

Like all good scientists, I didn't jump to conclusions; I started to look for evidence. I wasn't sure where to start, but it seemed sensible to go back and look again at that 'good man' Jesus and see where this would get me. So, over the course of a few months I read the Gospels and oh… oh… oh! I dashed into school and blurted out in a sewing lesson, 'You know all that stuff they used to tell us at Sunday school – all those fairy stories about God and Jesus – they're true – *really* true!' The teacher took me aside and said, 'Joanna, I think you have become a Christian.'

Science is essentially a systematic way of investigating the world in order to try and find out what is true – *really* true. It realises that, in the words of Jesus, 'the truth shall set you free'. Like me, it is not afraid to ask those awkward questions, but it is much humbler than I was about my multiplication tables. It realises that its models are provisional and that its knowledge has limits.

For most of my career I have been a scientist, working in the area of brain and behaviour. I have done research on the way the brain enables us to think and to feel emotions, and at the moment I am doing research into the way the brain enables us to pray or have mystical experiences. I am passionate about integrating science and faith – showing how they are two sides of the same coin.

I've been able to pursue a career in science because I decided to study science at A level. I can remember it clearly, sitting in my school library struggling to fill in the subject choice form. It was difficult because, if anything, I preferred and was better at humanities. As I struggled I prayed; this is what came to mind: 'When we study great literature, art or history, we study what humans have made and done; when we study the created world we study what God has made and done.'

For me, science is a way to come close to the mind of God – it's theology. It's also a form of worship because wonder is appreciative and wondering is a kind of attentive looking and listening. Jesus tells us to 'consider the lilies' – to be appreciative and observant. He also says, 'Let anyone with ears to hear listen!' As an adolescent, my ears heard '13 x 13' and, like the young Samuel, my reply was and still is, 'Here I am!'

Index of activities

Index of Bible verses

Index of themes

Glossary

Many scientific terms are described in the 'Big thinking' sections of each experiment. For more information, check the internet, which has some simple scientific explanations!

A few terms that occur across several experiments are described here.

Air resistance
The force exerted by air as an object moves through it.

Atom
The smallest component of a substance. See pp. 104–105.

Buoyancy force
A force exerted on an object due to it having a different density to the fluid it is immersed in. See pp. 24, 30.

Catalyst
A chemical substance that assists two other materials to react together, but is not used up in the reaction itself.

Centrifugal force
The force felt by a rotating object, pushing it out from the central point around which it is rotating.

Convection current
The motion of a fluid/air, due to it being hotter/less dense or colder/more dense than the surrounding fluid.

Density
The amount of a material in a unit volume.

Diameter
The distance across a circle through its central point.

Diffraction
The bending of waves around the edge of an obstacle that has a similar size to the wave length of the wave. Different colours of light are bent by different amounts.

Electron
A sub-atomic particle with a negative electrical charge.

Element
A specific substance with the same number of protons in the atom's nucleus. Currently we know 118 elements exist, of which 98 are found in nature, the rest only being made in laboratories.

Fine tuning
The suggestion that the laws of physics appear just right for life to emerge within the universe.

Frequency
The number of times a wave oscillates in a second.

Friction
The force exerted when two objects move against each other.

Ion
An atom that has lost or gained electrons so that it has an overall positive or negative charge.

Kinetic energy
The energy of an object due to its motion.

Molecule
The smallest particle of a substance, composed of a collection of atoms.

Neutron
A sub-atomic particle with no electrical charge.

Particle
A small piece of a substance. This can refer to things of many different sizes, such as atoms through to pollen grains.

Photon
A particle of light.

Polymer
A long molecule of a substance composed of repeating units of smaller molecules.

Potential energy
The energy stored within an object, or by an object due to its position relative to another object, which might be converted to other forms of energy, such as heat or motion.

Proton
A sub-atomic particle with a positive electrical charge.

Retina
The back part of the eye on which the lens of the eye creates an image.

Spectrum
The range of different wave lengths of light.

Ultraviolet (UV) light
Light whose wave length is shorter than that of blue light that we can see with our eyes. It causes skin to tan and burn.

Vacuum
A volume of space with no material or air in it.

Variable
The different factors that might change the result of an experiment.

What do you think of *Messy Church Does Science*?

We hope you have enjoyed using the ideas and experiments in *Messy Church Does Science*. This book is part of a larger project, which aims to demonstrate that science and faith are complementary and to help children and adults alike appreciate the wonder of creation. Here at The Bible Reading Fellowship (BRF), the home of Messy Church, we want to make sure that *Messy Church Does Science* is the best it can be. To help, could you spare a few minutes to give us your thoughts?

Below is a short feedback form for Messy Church Does Science activity leaders and a second feedback form for Messy Church families. Please feel free to detach these pages and photocopy them as needed. Any completed forms can be scanned and emailed to **enquiries@brf.org.uk** or you can post them to:

Messy Church team
The Bible Reading Fellowship
BRF, 15 The Chambers, Vineyard
Abingdon OX14 3FE

The surveys are also available online at **www.messychurch.org.uk/science**.

Thank you for your help.

Interview form for *Messy Church Does Science* activity leaders

Name .... Messy Church ....

Your own level of scientific qualification ....

How often has your team held science-based activities in your Messy Church before now?

Most times ☐   Often ☐   Occasionally ☐   Never ☐

Why? *Please tick any that apply:*

☐ We've always appreciated science

☐ We've never thought of using science

☐ We've always felt science and faith can inform each other

☐ We've never felt science and faith can inform each other

☐ We've always felt confident about science

☐ We've never felt confident about science

☐ We have people with the right skills to lead science activities

☐ We don't have anyone with the right skills to lead science activities

☐ We've always felt science is fun

☐ We've always felt science is too dangerous

How often are you likely to hold science activities now that you have this resource?

Much more often ☐   Often ☐   Occasionally ☐   Never ☐   No change ☐

How did you feel about the level of scientific explanation for the activities?

Just right ☐   Too advanced ☐   Too basic ☐

How did you feel about the level of the 'God' explanation for the activities?

Just right ☐   Too advanced ☐   Too basic ☐

Has using *Messy Church Does Science* had any of these effects on you and your team?

We feel more confident to use science activities:

Yes ☐   No ☐   Unsure ☐

We feel better able to explain science activities:

Yes ☐   No ☐   Unsure ☐

We are more excited about using science at Messy Church:

Yes ☐   No ☐   Unsure ☐

After taking part in a *Messy Church Does Science* activity, are you more likely or less likely to:

	More likely	Less likely	About the same
Watch films or TV programmes on the theme of the activity?	☐	☐	☐
Read articles or books on the theme of the activity?	☐	☐	☐
Want to visit a museum or nature reserve to find out more about the theme of the activity?	☐	☐	☐

Would you recommend *Messy Church Does Science* to another Messy Church leader?

Yes ☐   No ☐

Other comments:

Interview form for Messy Church families

Name .... Messy Church ....

How did you enjoy the *Messy Church Does Science* activity?

A lot ☐   It was okay ☐   Not much ☐   Not at all ☐

What was the best *Messy Church Does Science* activity you've done?

Can you explain what you saw?

What Bible story did it remind you of?

What did you discover about God through the activity? (Or what did it remind you about God?)

Before you came to Messy Church, did you think science and Christianity went well together?

Yes ☐   No ☐   Not sure ☐

Now you've done science at Messy Church, do you think science and Christianity go well together?

Yes ☐   No ☐   Not sure ☐

Have you come across the *Messy Church Does Science* at home activities?

Yes ☐   No ☐

Have you used any *Messy Church Does Science* at home activities?

Yes ☐   No ☐

Would you like to use them in the future?

Yes ☐   No ☐   Not sure ☐

Messy Church is part of The Bible Reading Fellowship (BRF), a Registered Charity (233280)

After taking part in a *Messy Church Does Science* activity, are you more likely or less likely to:

	More likely	Less likely	About the same
Watch films or TV programmes on the theme of the activity?	☐	☐	☐
Read articles or books on the theme of the activity?	☐	☐	☐
Want to visit a museum or nature reserve to find out more about the theme of the activity?	☐	☐	☐

Would you like your Messy Church to do *Messy Church Does Science* activities again?

Yes ☐   No ☐

Would you invite a friend to come and do *Messy Church Does Science*?

Yes ☐   No ☐

Other comments:

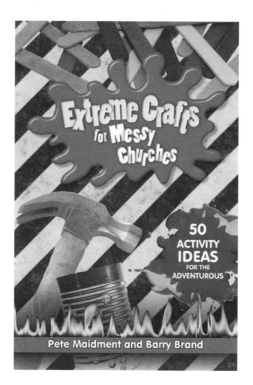

In this book, Pete Maidment and Barry Brand provide over 50 new activities for Messy Church sessions, carefully crafted to appeal to male as well as female participants at Messy Church. They challenge the assumption that Messy Church 'isn't really for men or boys' and offer approaches for Messy Churches to engage men and boys in an intentional way, providing inspiration for creating a Messy Church that men and boys, as well as women and girls, will love to be part of.

Extreme Crafts for Messy Churches
50 activity ideas for the adventurous
Pete Maidment, Barry Brand
978 0 85746 162 9 £7.99

brfonline.org.uk

Transforming
lives and communities

Christian growth and understanding of the Bible

Resourcing individuals, groups and leaders in churches for their own spiritual journey and for their ministry

Church outreach in the local community

Offering three programmes that churches are embracing to great effect as they seek to engage with their local communities and transform lives

Teaching Christianity in primary schools

Working with children and teachers to explore Christianity creatively and confidently

Children's and family ministry

Working with churches and families to explore Christianity creatively and bring the Bible alive

Visit **brf.org.uk** for more information on BRF's work

brf.org.uk

The Bible Reading Fellowship (BRF) is a Registered Charity (No. 233280)